EASY TO LEARN,
DIFFICULT TO MASTER

EASY TO LEARN, DIFFICULT TO MASTER

PONG, ATARI, AND THE DAWN OF THE VIDEO GAME

DAVID KUSHNER

KOREN SHADMI

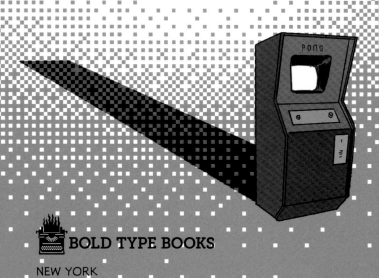

BOLD TYPE BOOKS

NEW YORK

BOLD TYPE BOOKS
116 EAST 16TH STREET, 8TH FLOOR NEW YORK, NY 10003
WWW.BOLDTYPEBOOKS.ORG
@BOLDTYPEBOOKS
PRINTED IN CANADA

FIRST EDITION: SEPTEMBER 2022

PUBLISHED BY BOLD TYPE BOOKS, AN IMPRINT OF PERSEUS BOOKS, LLC,
A SUBSIDIARY OF HACHETTE BOOK GROUP, INC.
BOLD TYPE BOOKS IS A CO-PUBLISHING VENTURE OF THE TYPE MEDIA CENTER
AND PERSEUS BOOKS.

THE HACHETTE SPEAKERS BUREAU PROVIDES A WIDE RANGE OF
AUTHORS FOR SPEAKING EVENTS. TO FIND OUT MORE, GO TO
WWW.HACHETTESPEAKERSBUREAU.COM OR CALL (866) 376-6591.

THE PUBLISHER IS NOT RESPONSIBLE FOR WEBSITES (OR THEIR CONTENT)
THAT ARE NOT OWNED BY THE PUBLISHER.

PRINT BOOK INTERIOR DESIGN BY KOREN SHADMI

LIBRARY OF CONGRESS CONTROL NUMBER: 2021951428

ISBNS: 9781568588766 (PAPERBACK), 9781568588759 (EBOOK)

FRI

EASY TO LEARN, DIFFICULT TO MASTER IS INSPIRED BY MY ARTICLE "SEX, DRUGS, AND VIDEO GAMES: THE UNTOLD STORY OF ATARI," WHICH APPEARED IN PLAY-BOY IN JULY 2012. THE DIALOGUE AND SCENES ARE DRAWN FROM MY EXTENSIVE INTERVIEWS WITH NOLAN BUSHNELL, RALPH BAER, AND THEIR COLLEAGUES; AS WELL COURT DOCUMENTS; BAER'S MEMOIR, VIDEOGAMES: IN THE BEGINNING; AND OTHER REPORTING. SOME SCENES HAVE BEEN FICTIONALIZED AND CERTAIN NAMES HAVE BEEN CHANGED.

EASY TO LEARN, DIFFICULT TO MASTER

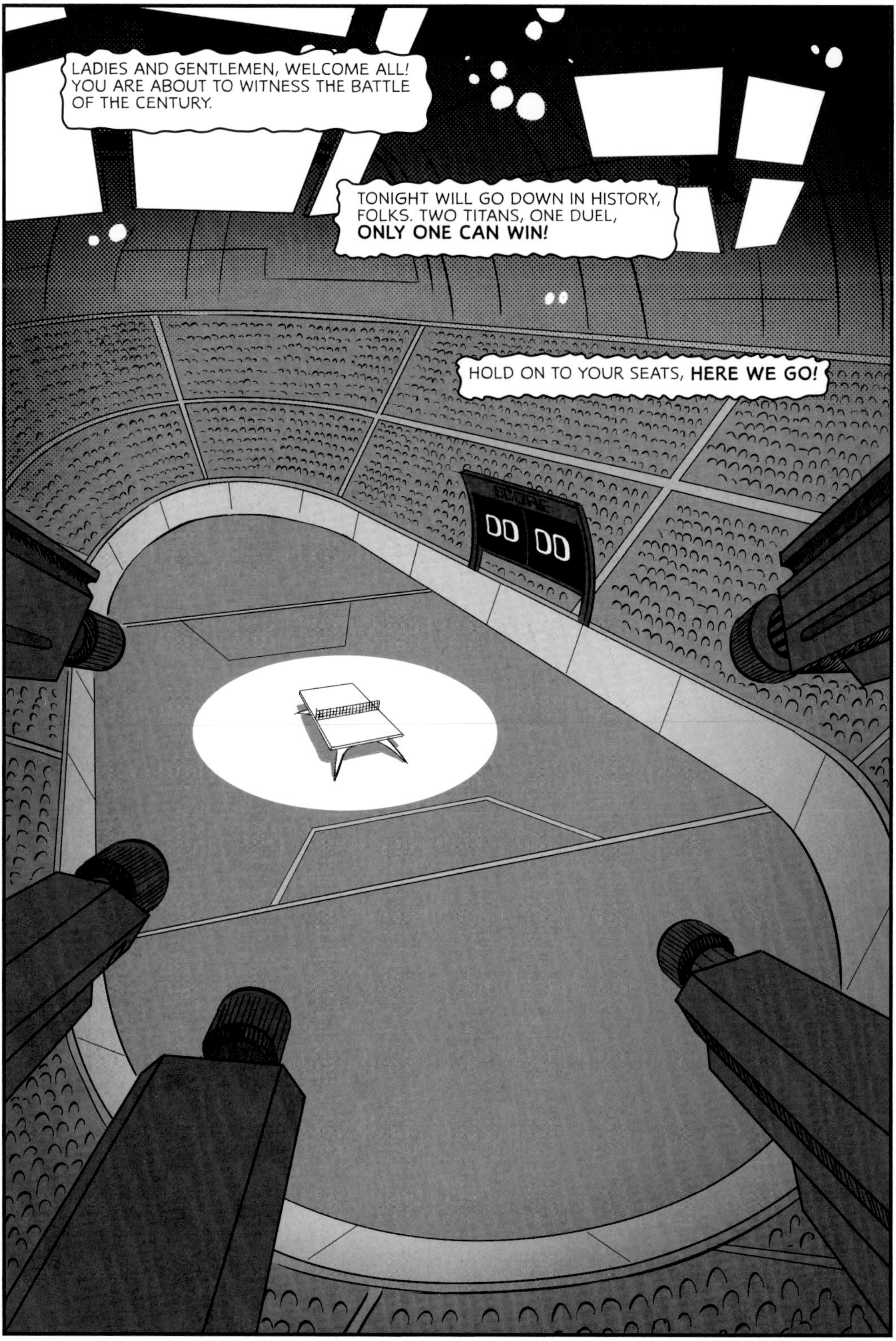
LADIES AND GENTLEMEN, WELCOME ALL! YOU ARE ABOUT TO WITNESS THE BATTLE OF THE CENTURY.
TONIGHT WILL GO DOWN IN HISTORY, FOLKS. TWO TITANS, ONE DUEL, **ONLY ONE CAN WIN!**
HOLD ON TO YOUR SEATS, **HERE WE GO!**
SCORE
00 00

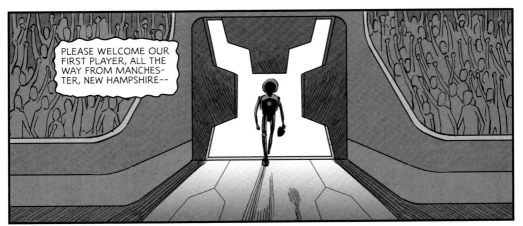

PLEASE WELCOME OUR FIRST PLAYER, ALL THE WAY FROM MANCHESTER, NEW HAMPSHIRE--

RAAAAAAALPH BAER!

BEHOLD! I AM THE FATHER OF VIDEO GAMES!

BOK!

OH HO HO! THAT MUST BE OUR OTHER COMPETITOR, RALPH'S BITTER RIVAL.

JETTING IN FROM HIS BEAUTIFUL MANSION IN LOS ANGELES, CALIFORNIA:

NOOOOLAN BUSHNELL!

GREETINGS, EVERYONE. THE TRUE FATHER OF VIDEO GAMES RIGHT HERE!

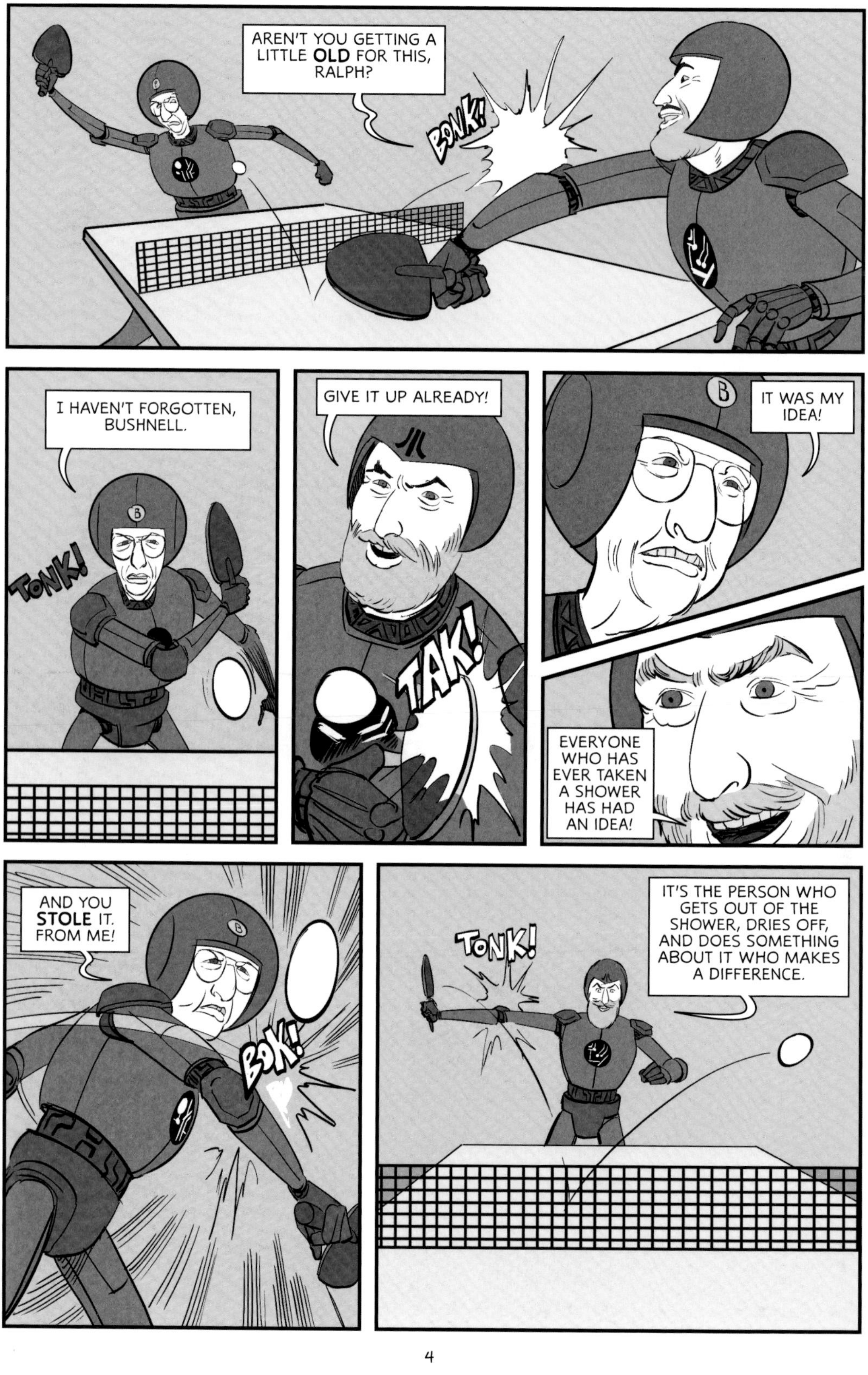
AREN'T YOU GETTING A LITTLE **OLD** FOR THIS, RALPH?
BONK!
I HAVEN'T FORGOTTEN, BUSHNELL.
TONK!
GIVE IT UP ALREADY!
TAK!
IT WAS MY IDEA!
EVERYONE WHO HAS EVER TAKEN A SHOWER HAS HAD AN IDEA!
AND YOU **STOLE** IT. FROM ME!
BOK!
TONK!
IT'S THE PERSON WHO GETS OUT OF THE SHOWER, DRIES OFF, AND DOES SOMETHING ABOUT IT WHO MAKES A DIFFERENCE.

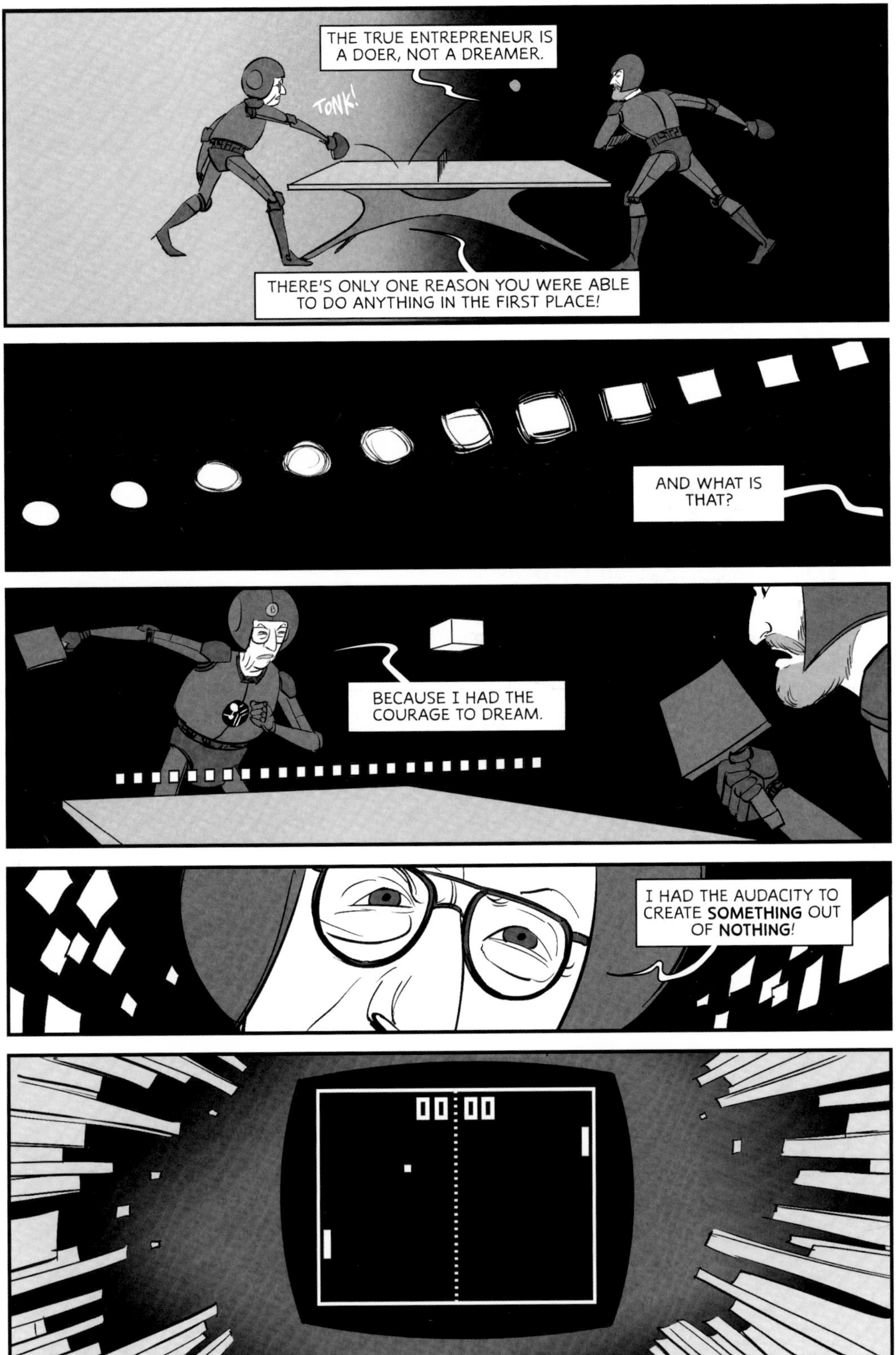
THE TRUE ENTREPRENEUR IS A DOER, NOT A DREAMER.
TONK!
THERE'S ONLY ONE REASON YOU WERE ABLE TO DO ANYTHING IN THE FIRST PLACE!
AND WHAT IS THAT?
BECAUSE I HAD THE COURAGE TO DREAM.
I HAD THE AUDACITY TO CREATE **SOMETHING** OUT OF **NOTHING**!
00 00

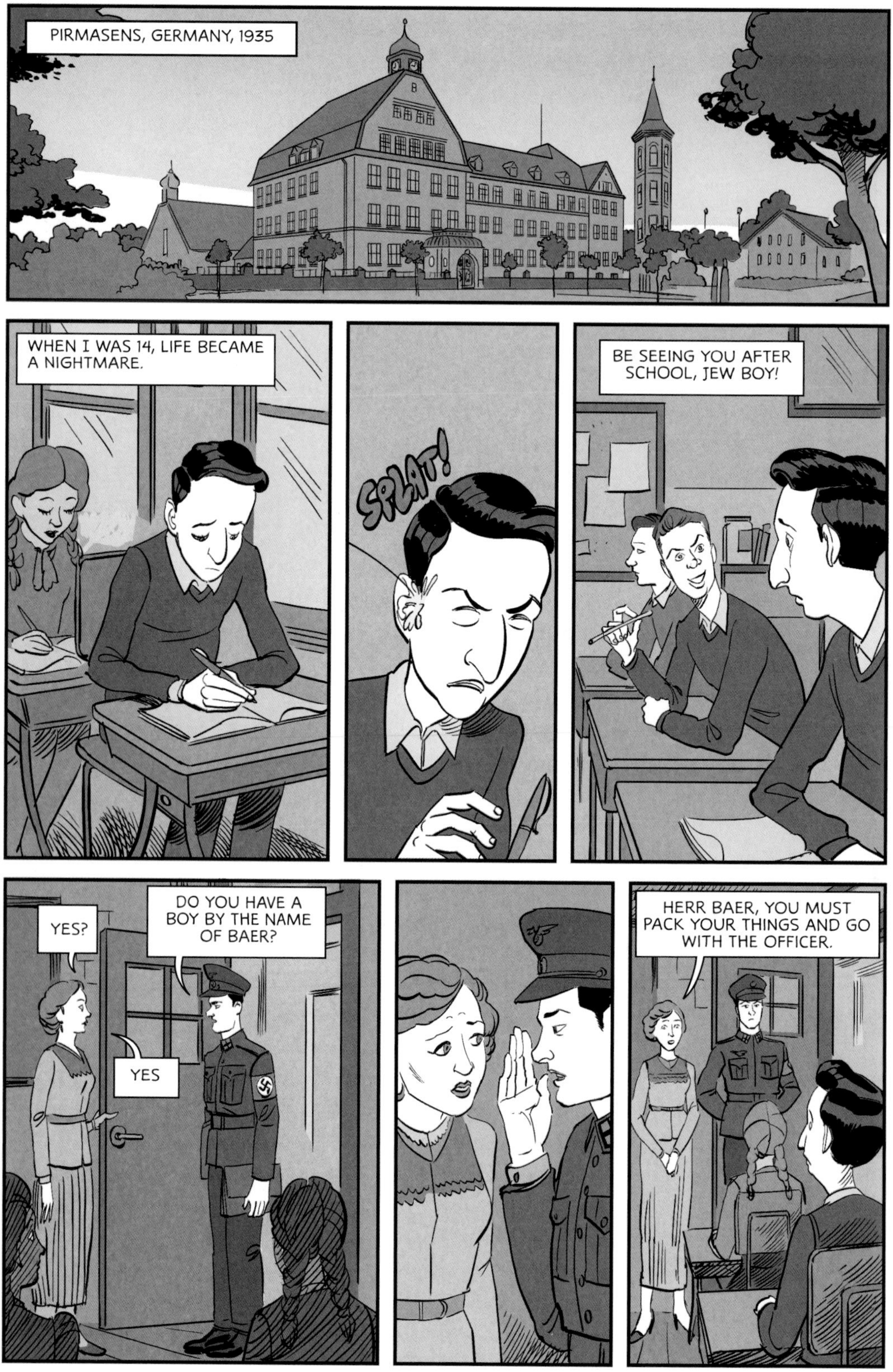
PIRMASENS, GERMANY, 1935
WHEN I WAS 14, LIFE BECAME A NIGHTMARE.
SPLAT!
BE SEEING YOU AFTER SCHOOL, JEW BOY!
YES?
DO YOU HAVE A BOY BY THE NAME OF BAER?
YES
HERR BAER, YOU MUST PACK YOUR THINGS AND GO WITH THE OFFICER.

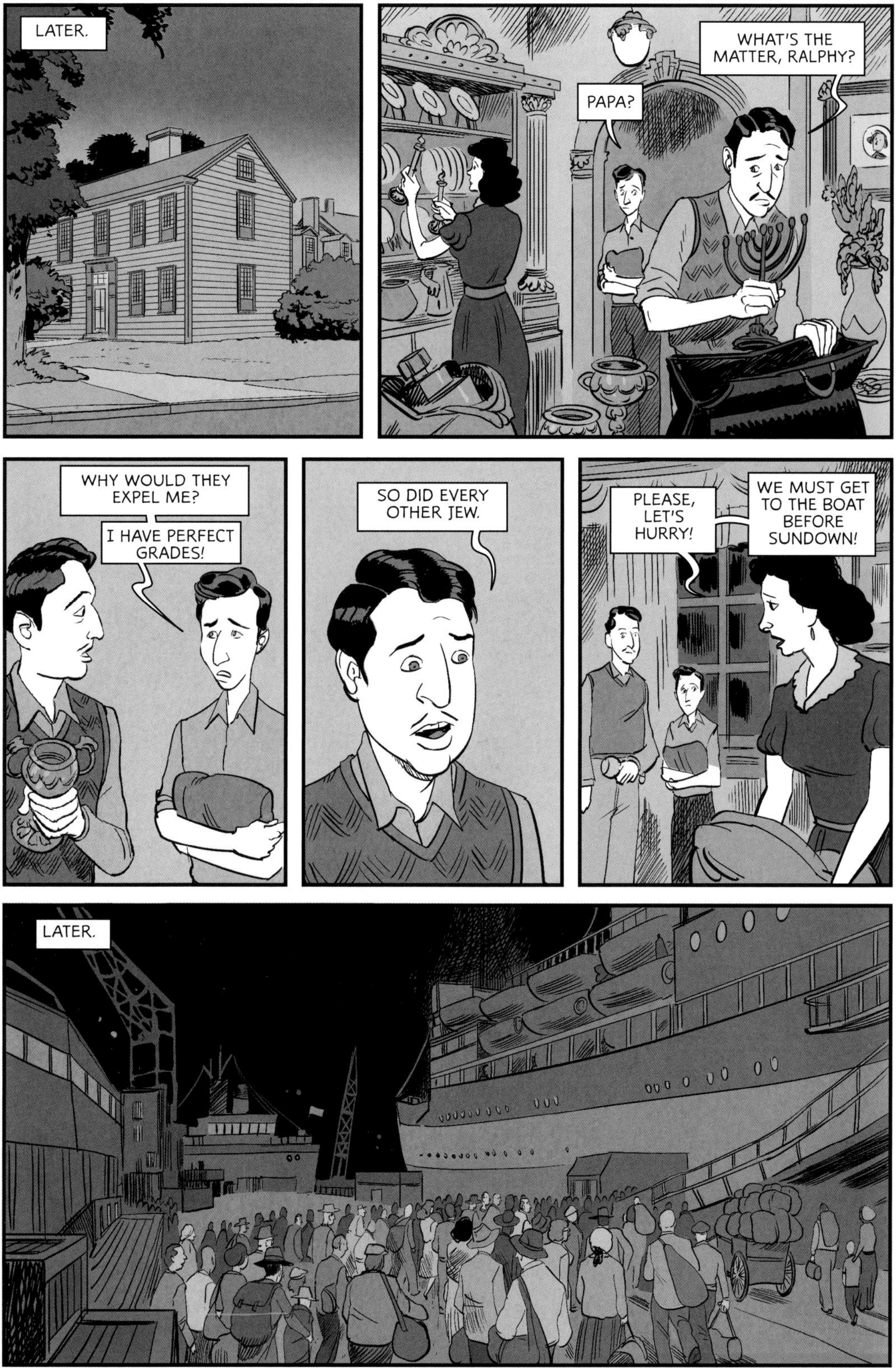
LATER.
PAPA?
WHAT'S THE MATTER, RALPHY?
WHY WOULD THEY EXPEL ME?
I HAVE PERFECT GRADES!
SO DID EVERY OTHER JEW.
PLEASE, LET'S HURRY!
WE MUST GET TO THE BOAT BEFORE SUNDOWN!
LATER.

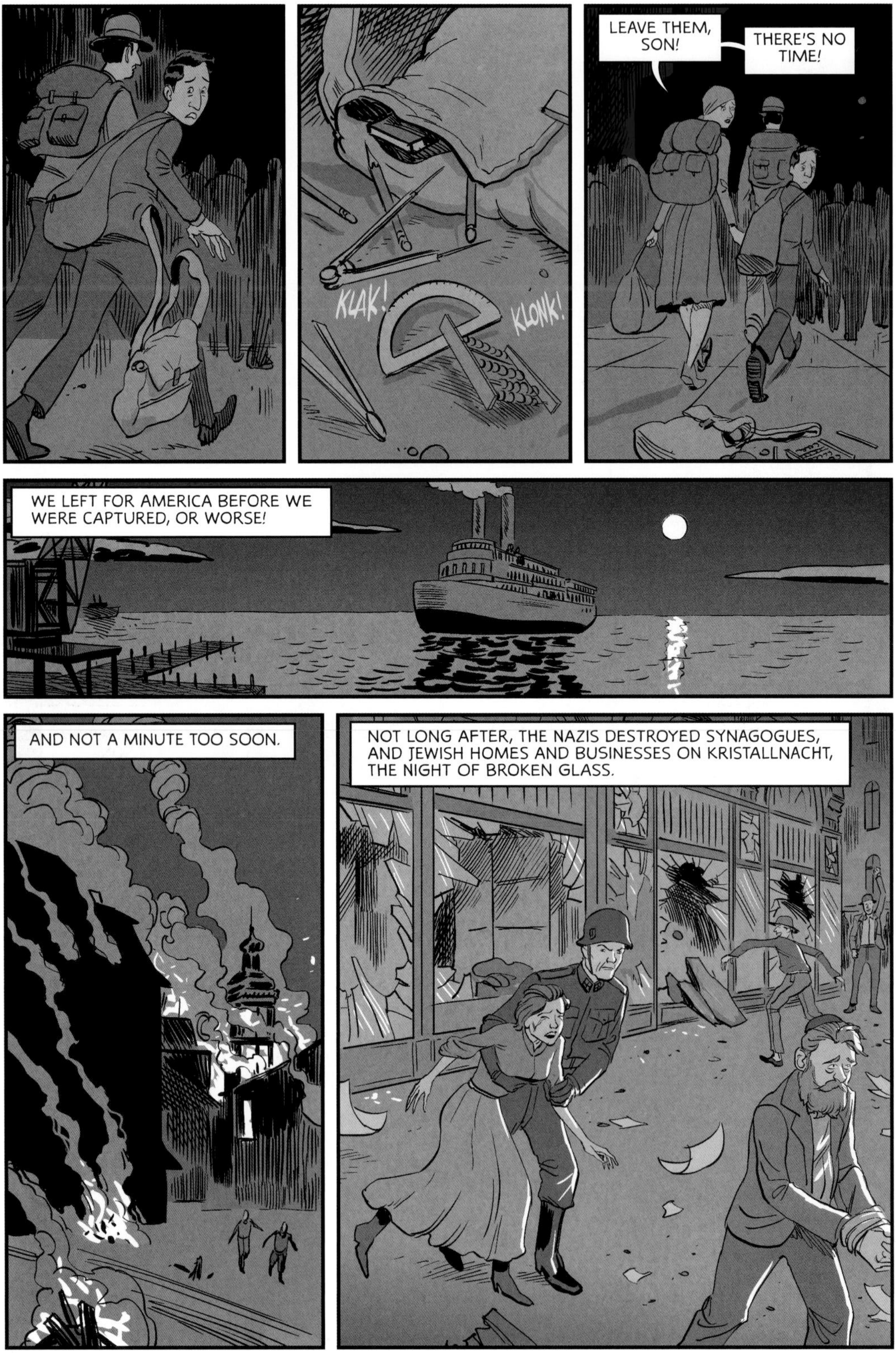
KLAK!
KLONK!
LEAVE THEM, SON!
THERE'S NO TIME!
WE LEFT FOR AMERICA BEFORE WE WERE CAPTURED, OR WORSE!
AND NOT A MINUTE TOO SOON.
NOT LONG AFTER, THE NAZIS DESTROYED SYNAGOGUES, AND JEWISH HOMES AND BUSINESSES ON KRISTALLNACHT, THE NIGHT OF BROKEN GLASS.

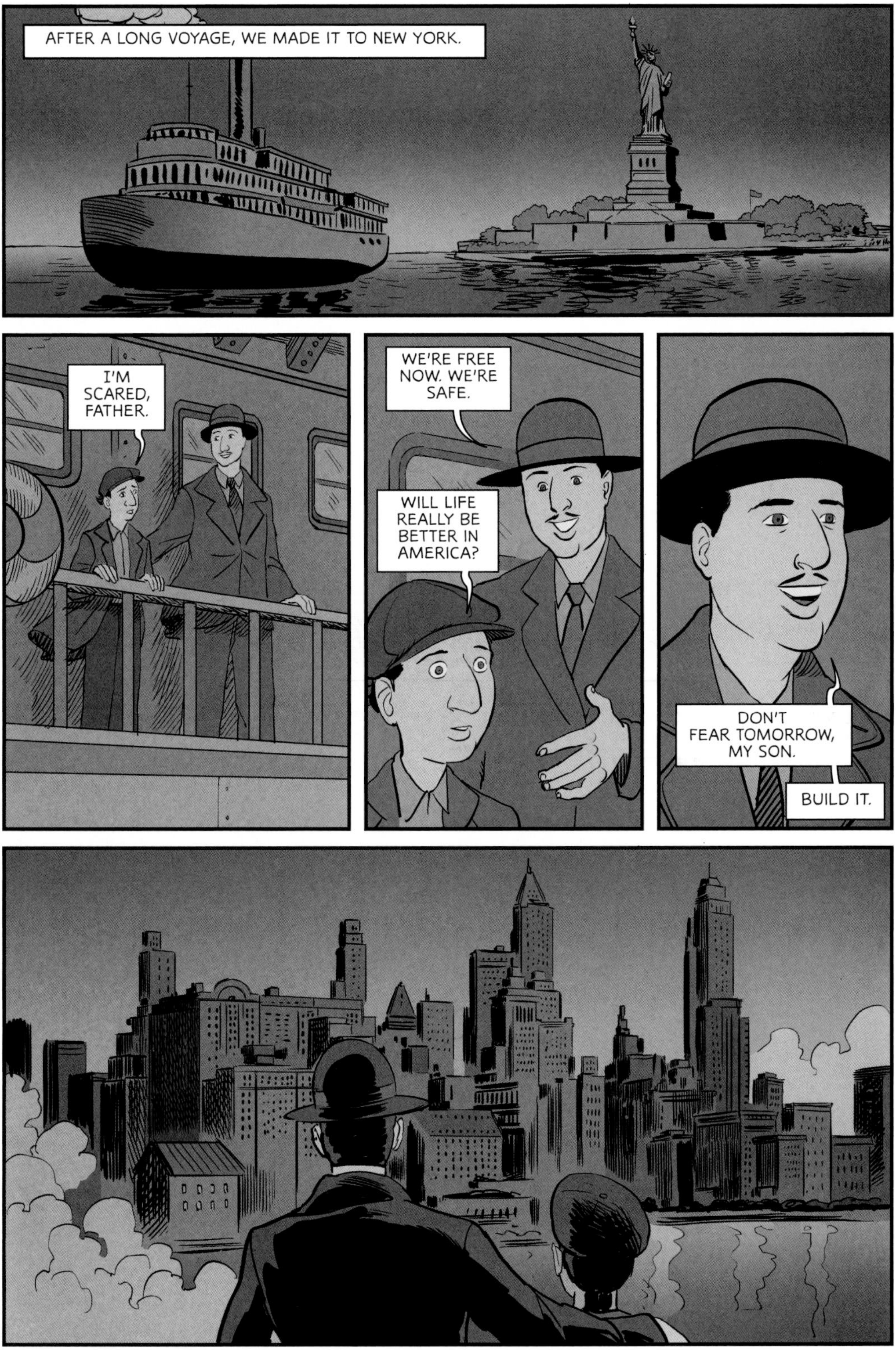
AFTER A LONG VOYAGE, WE MADE IT TO NEW YORK.
I'M SCARED, FATHER.
WE'RE FREE NOW. WE'RE SAFE.
WILL LIFE REALLY BE BETTER IN AMERICA?
DON'T FEAR TOMORROW, MY SON.
BUILD IT.

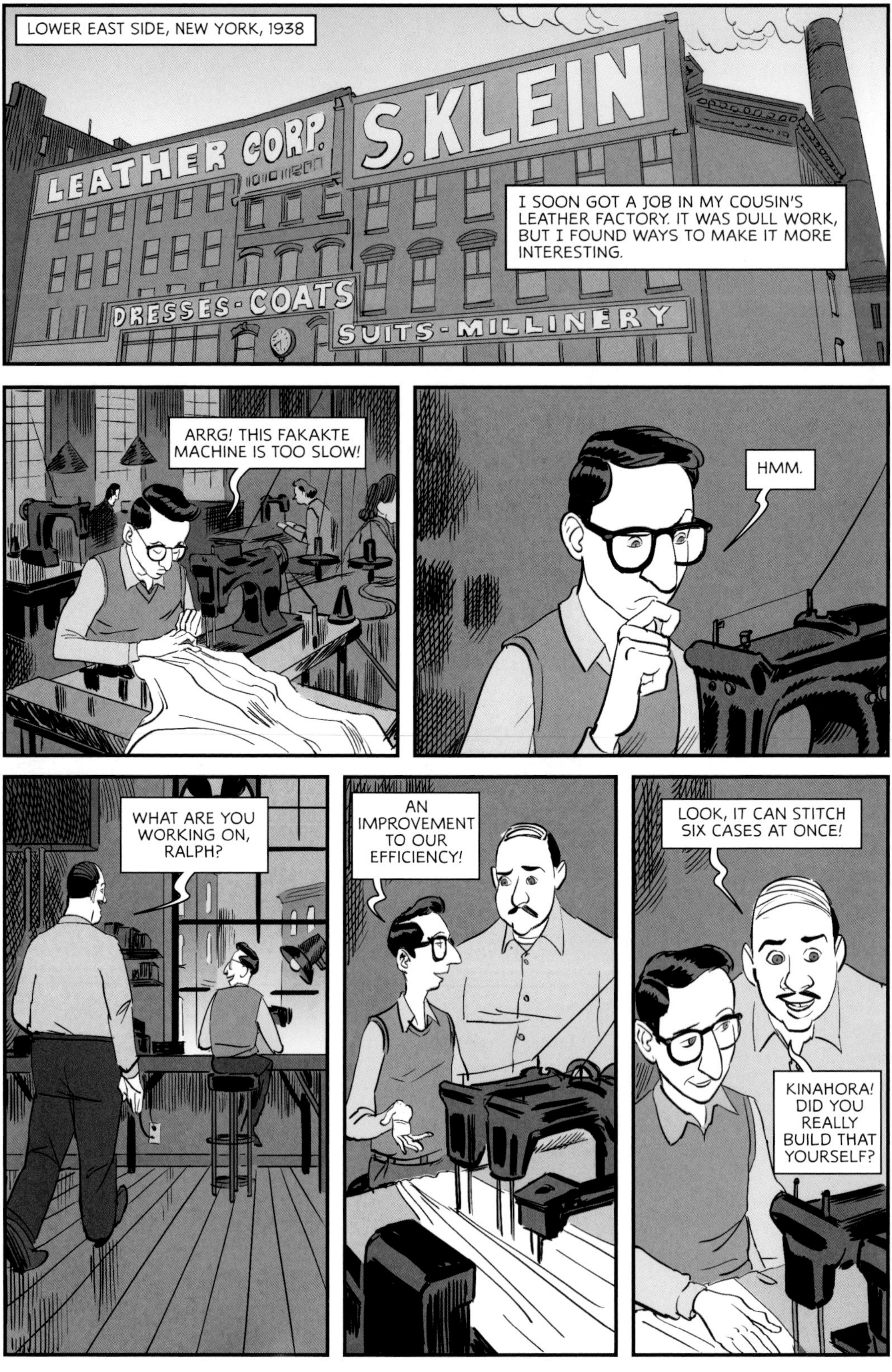
LOWER EAST SIDE, NEW YORK, 1938
LEATHER CORP.
S. KLEIN
I SOON GOT A JOB IN MY COUSIN'S LEATHER FACTORY. IT WAS DULL WORK, BUT I FOUND WAYS TO MAKE IT MORE INTERESTING.
DRESSES-COATS
SUITS-MILLINERY
ARRG! THIS FAKAKTE MACHINE IS TOO SLOW!
HMM.
WHAT ARE YOU WORKING ON, RALPH?
AN IMPROVEMENT TO OUR EFFICIENCY!
LOOK, IT CAN STITCH SIX CASES AT ONCE!
KINAHORA! DID YOU REALLY BUILD THAT YOURSELF?

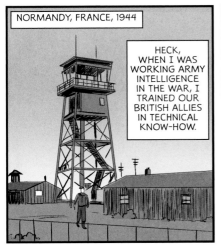

NORMANDY, FRANCE, 1944

HECK, WHEN I WAS WORKING ARMY INTELLIGENCE IN THE WAR, I TRAINED OUR BRITISH ALLIES IN TECHNICAL KNOW-HOW.

YOU NEED A DIFFERENT TRANSISTOR OVER HERE.

LATER.

I WISH I HAD A BOOK, OR SOMETHING!

I'M TIRED OF NAPPING...

DO YOU GUYS NEED THAT OLD GERMAN MINE DETECTOR IN THERE?

IT'S ALL YOURS, RALPH.

LATER STILL.

HUH?

I TURNED IT INTO A RADIO!

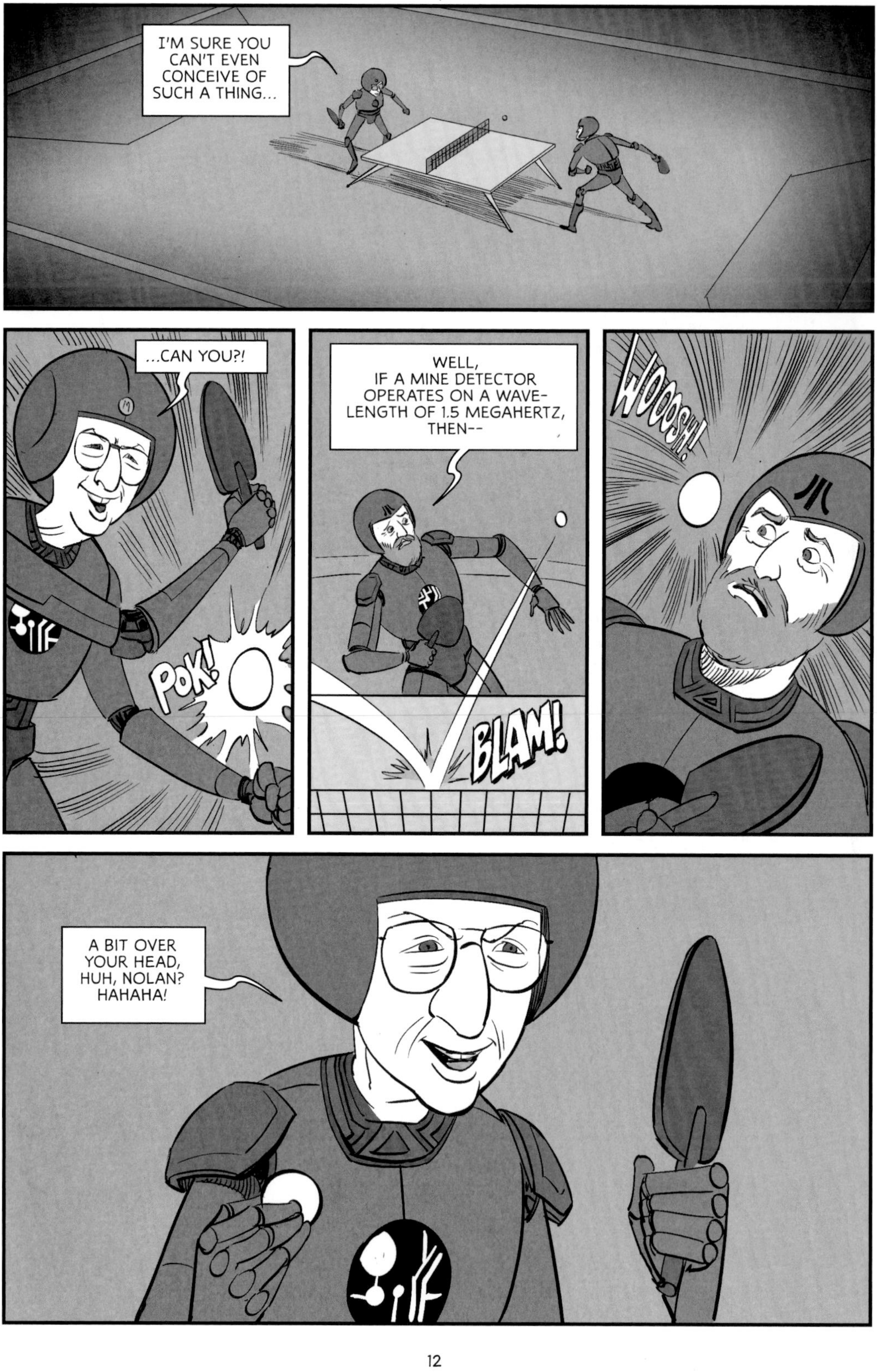
I'M SURE YOU CAN'T EVEN CONCEIVE OF SUCH A THING...
...CAN YOU?!
POK!
WELL, IF A MINE DETECTOR OPERATES ON A WAVE-LENGTH OF 1.5 MEGAHERTZ, THEN--
BLAM!
WOOOSH!
A BIT OVER YOUR HEAD, HUH, NOLAN? HAHAHA!

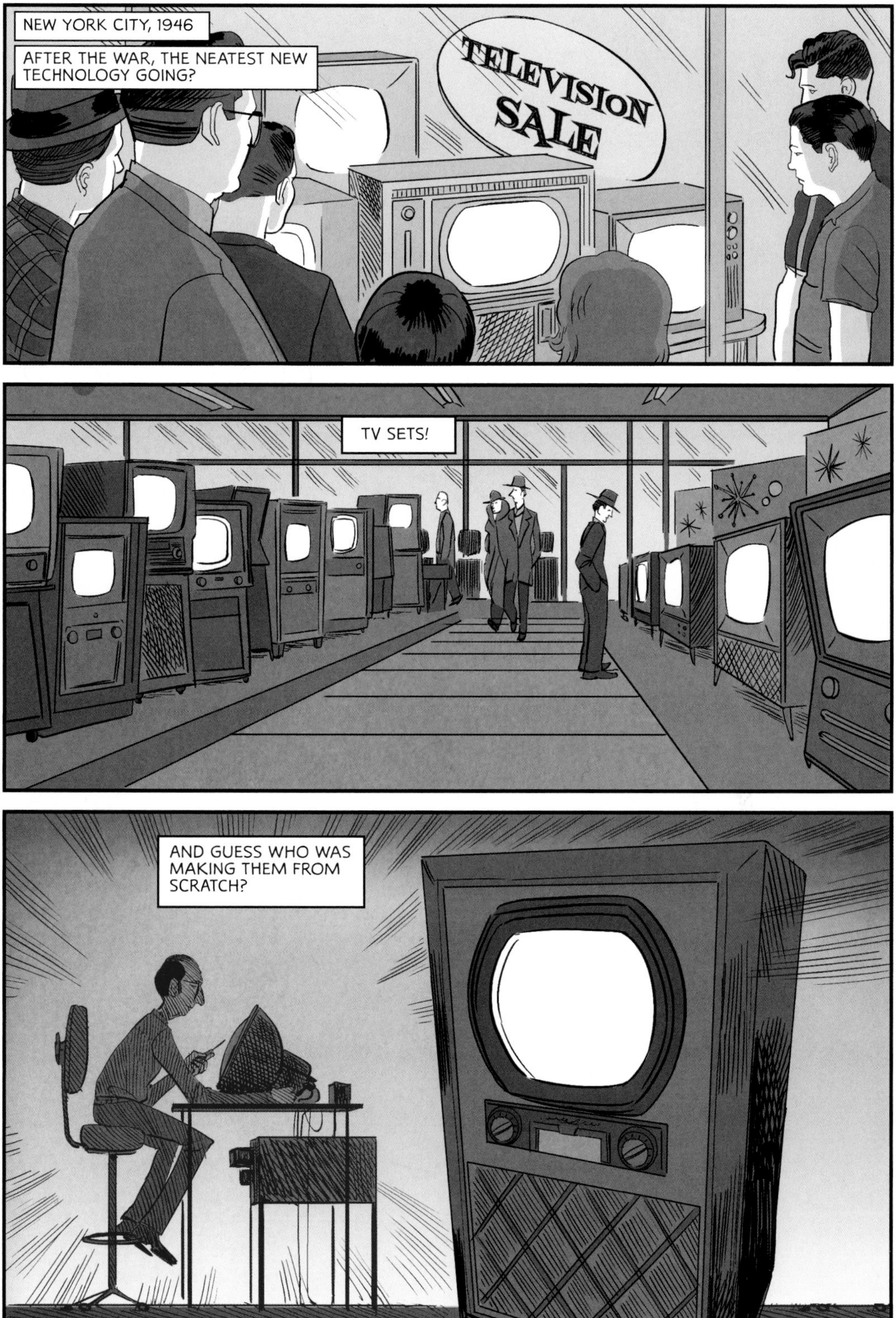
NEW YORK CITY, 1946
AFTER THE WAR, THE NEATEST NEW TECHNOLOGY GOING?
TELEVISION SALE
TV SETS!
AND GUESS WHO WAS MAKING THEM FROM SCRATCH?

LORAL CORPORATION, BRONX, NEW YORK, 1951

TO TEST THE SETS, WE'D MOVE DIFFERENT KINDS OF LINES.

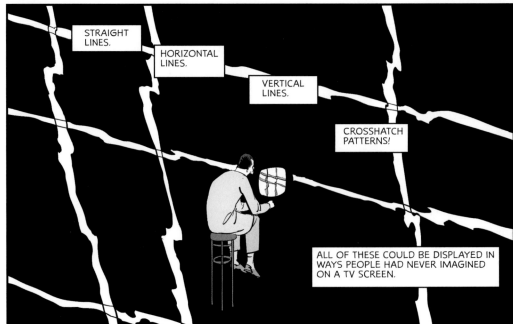

STRAIGHT LINES.

HORIZONTAL LINES.

VERTICAL LINES.

CROSSHATCH PATTERNS!

ALL OF THESE COULD BE DISPLAYED IN WAYS PEOPLE HAD NEVER IMAGINED ON A TV SCREEN.

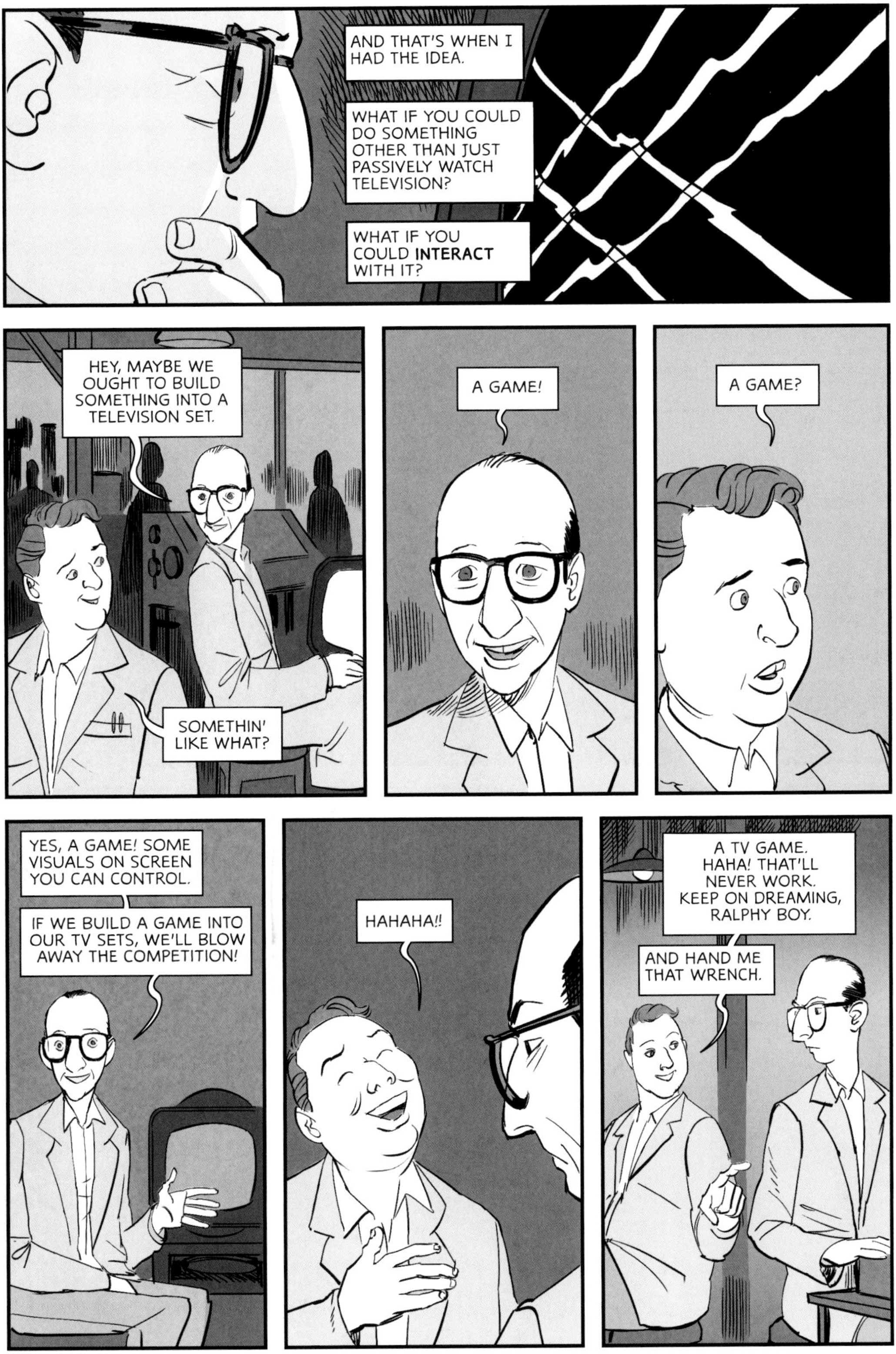
AND THAT'S WHEN I HAD THE IDEA.
WHAT IF YOU COULD DO SOMETHING OTHER THAN JUST PASSIVELY WATCH TELEVISION?
WHAT IF YOU COULD **INTERACT** WITH IT?
HEY, MAYBE WE OUGHT TO BUILD SOMETHING INTO A TELEVISION SET.
SOMETHIN' LIKE WHAT?
A GAME!
A GAME?
YES, A GAME! SOME VISUALS ON SCREEN YOU CAN CONTROL.
IF WE BUILD A GAME INTO OUR TV SETS, WE'LL BLOW AWAY THE COMPETITION!
HAHAHA!!
A TV GAME. HAHA! THAT'LL NEVER WORK. KEEP ON DREAMING, RALPHY BOY.
AND HAND ME THAT WRENCH.

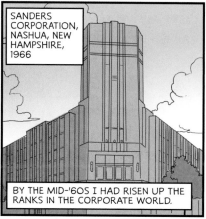

SANDERS CORPORATION, NASHUA, NEW HAMPSHIRE, 1966

BY THE MID-'60S I HAD RISEN UP THE RANKS IN THE CORPORATE WORLD.

I WAS OVERSEEING 500 ENGINEERS WORKING ON DISPLAY SYSTEMS FOR THE MILITARY.

AND I KNEW THE MARKET FOR TELEVISION WAS ONLY GOING TO GROW.

THERE WERE 198 MILLION TV SETS IN HOMES AROUND THE WORLD.

HOME TV
RADIOS & APPLIANCES

SYLVANIA
RADIO · TV

SYLVANIA TV

Emerson
RADIO · TV

DEFOREST
TRAINING INC
TV TECHNICIANS

AND THEY WERE BEGGING TO BE USED FOR SOMETHING OTHER THAN WATCHING COMMERCIAL TELEVISION BROADCASTS!

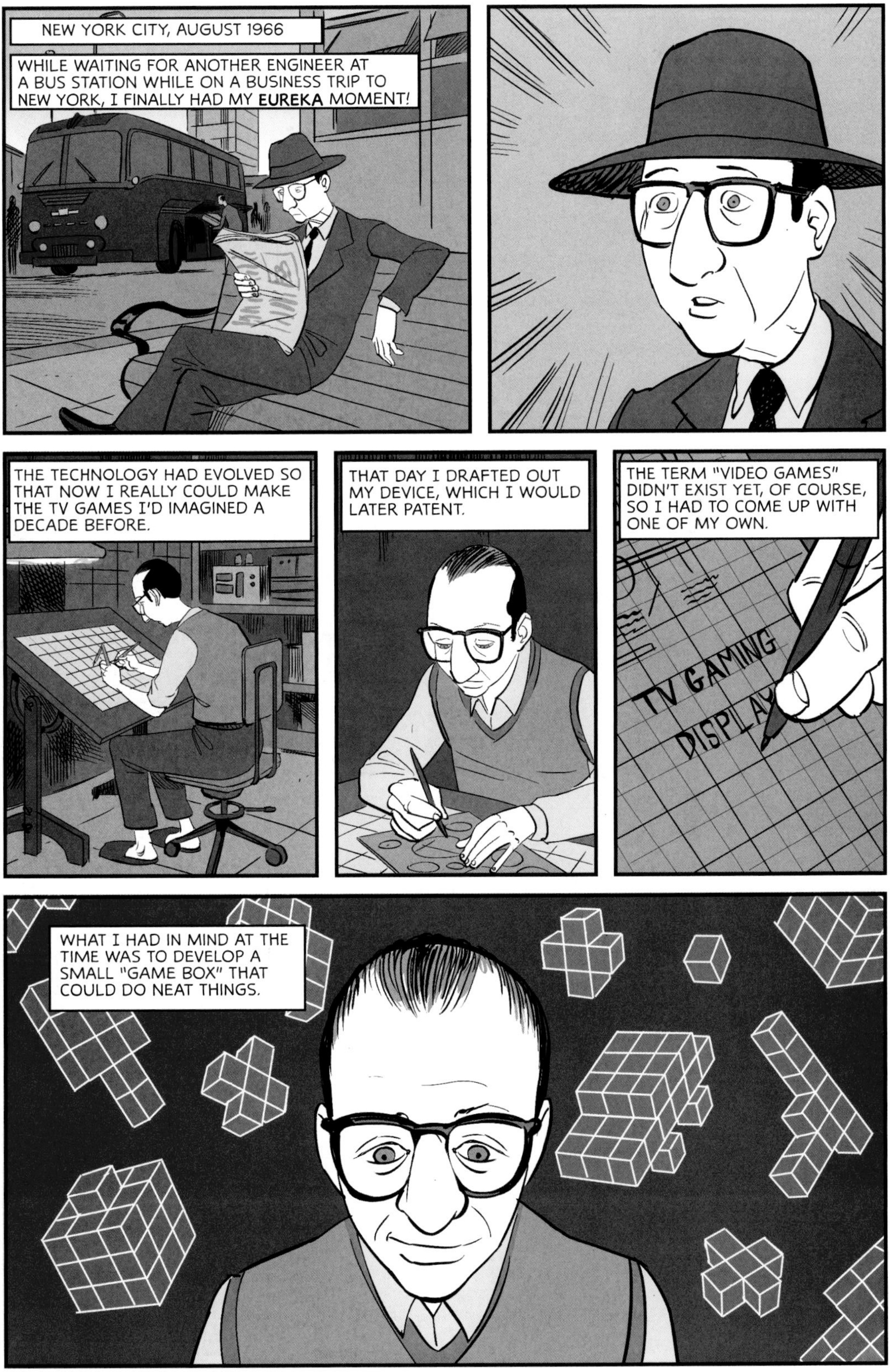
NEW YORK CITY, AUGUST 1966
WHILE WAITING FOR ANOTHER ENGINEER AT A BUS STATION WHILE ON A BUSINESS TRIP TO NEW YORK, I FINALLY HAD MY **EUREKA** MOMENT!
THE TECHNOLOGY HAD EVOLVED SO THAT NOW I REALLY COULD MAKE THE TV GAMES I'D IMAGINED A DECADE BEFORE.
THAT DAY I DRAFTED OUT MY DEVICE, WHICH I WOULD LATER PATENT.
THE TERM "VIDEO GAMES" DIDN'T EXIST YET, OF COURSE, SO I HAD TO COME UP WITH ONE OF MY OWN.
TV GAMING DISPLAY
WHAT I HAD IN MIND AT THE TIME WAS TO DEVELOP A SMALL "GAME BOX" THAT COULD DO NEAT THINGS.

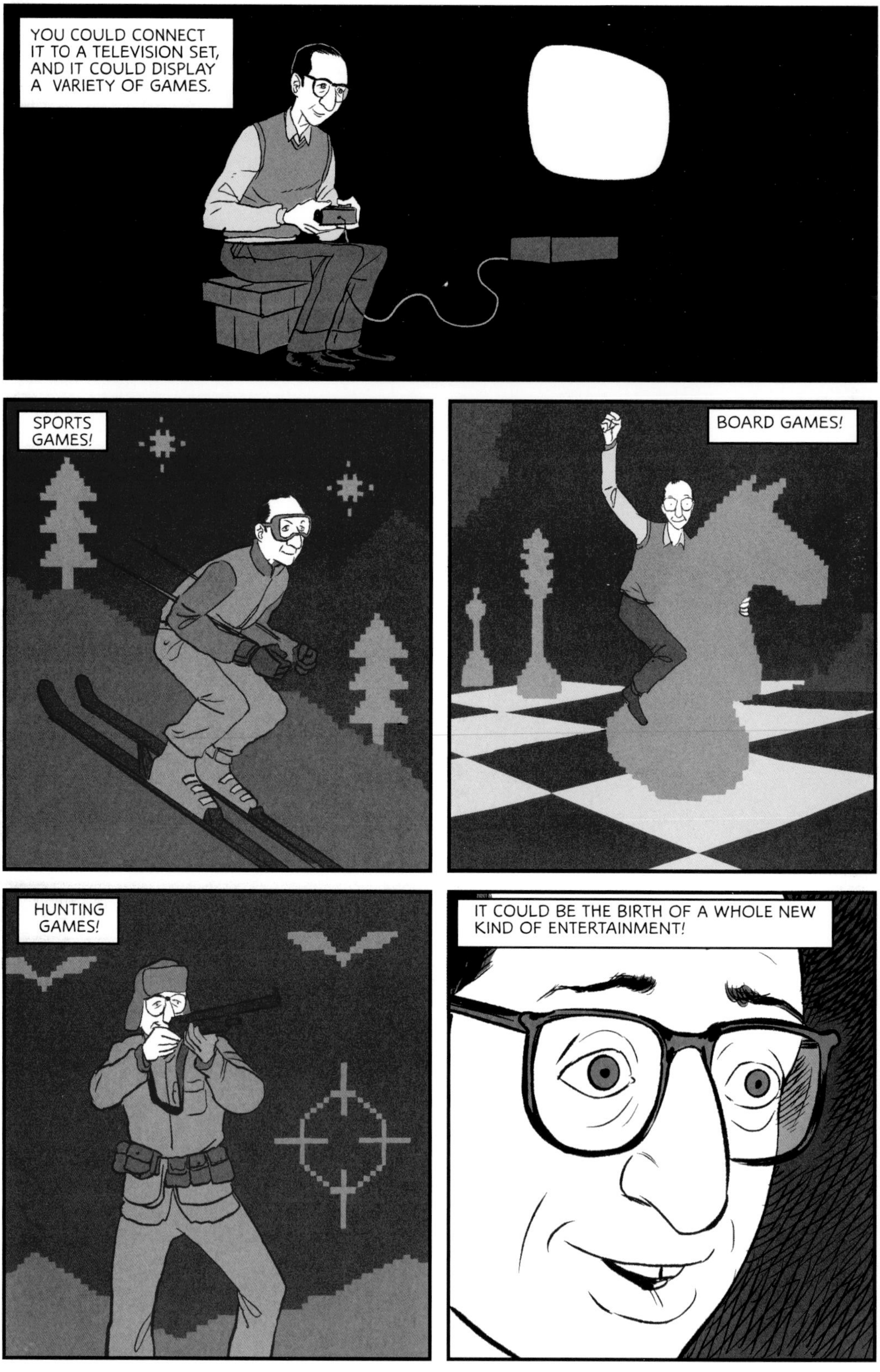
YOU COULD CONNECT IT TO A TELEVISION SET, AND IT COULD DISPLAY A VARIETY OF GAMES.
SPORTS GAMES!
BOARD GAMES!
HUNTING GAMES!
IT COULD BE THE BIRTH OF A WHOLE NEW KIND OF ENTERTAINMENT!

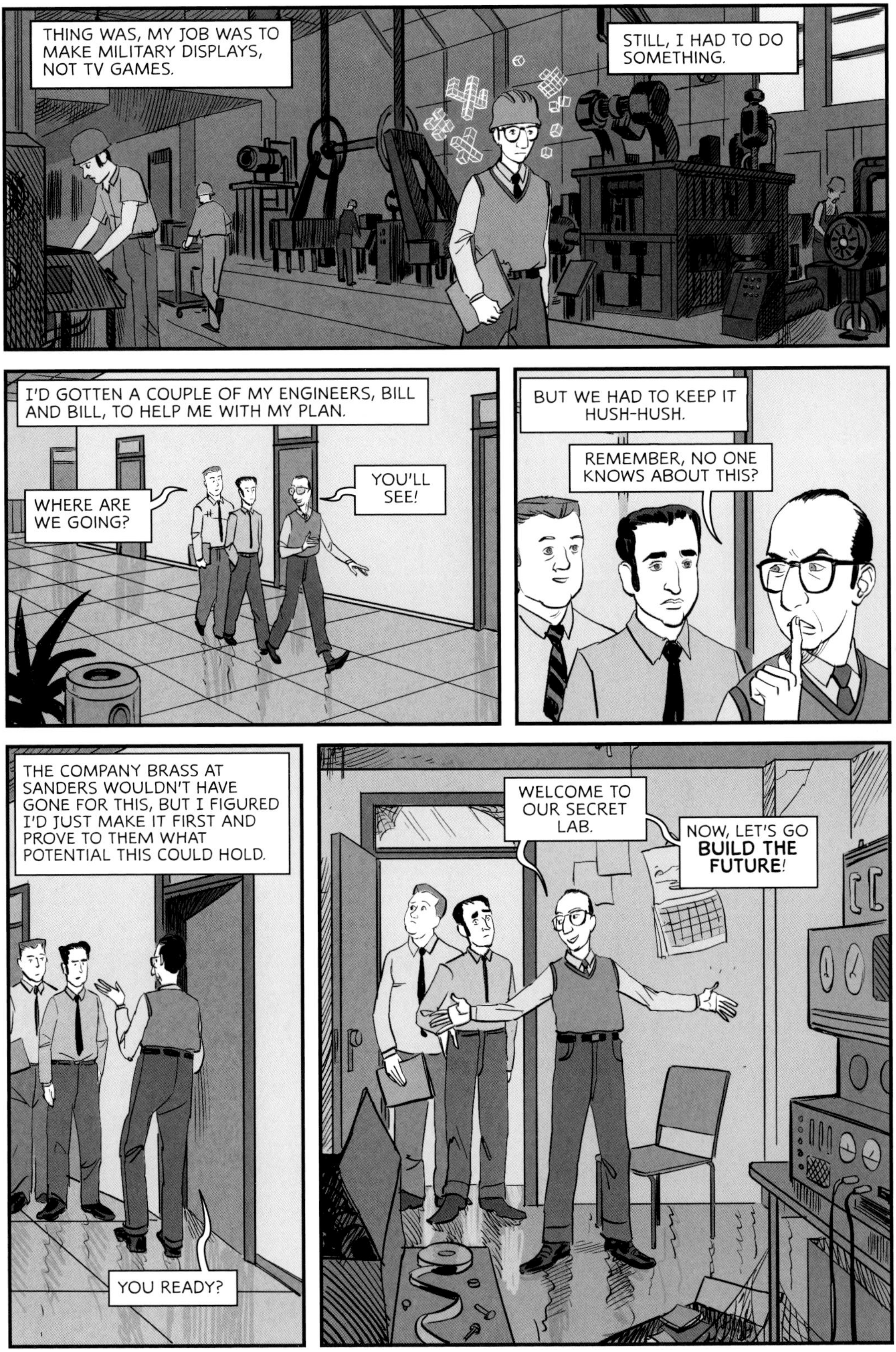
THING WAS, MY JOB WAS TO MAKE MILITARY DISPLAYS, NOT TV GAMES.
STILL, I HAD TO DO SOMETHING.
I'D GOTTEN A COUPLE OF MY ENGINEERS, BILL AND BILL, TO HELP ME WITH MY PLAN.
WHERE ARE WE GOING?
YOU'LL SEE!
BUT WE HAD TO KEEP IT HUSH-HUSH.
REMEMBER, NO ONE KNOWS ABOUT THIS?
THE COMPANY BRASS AT SANDERS WOULDN'T HAVE GONE FOR THIS, BUT I FIGURED I'D JUST MAKE IT FIRST AND PROVE TO THEM WHAT POTENTIAL THIS COULD HOLD.
YOU READY?
WELCOME TO OUR SECRET LAB.
NOW, LET'S GO **BUILD THE FUTURE**!

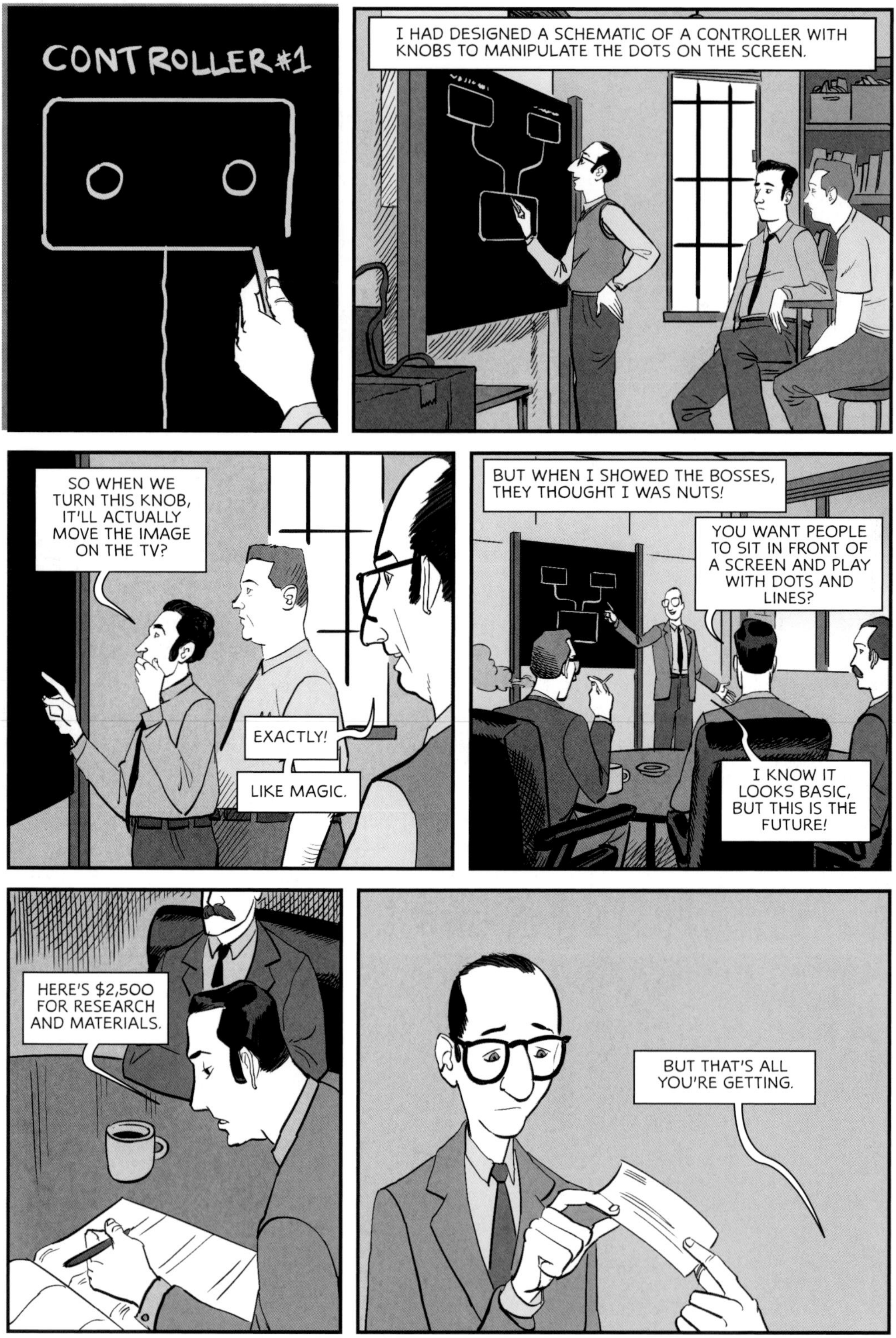
CONTROLLER #1
I HAD DESIGNED A SCHEMATIC OF A CONTROLLER WITH KNOBS TO MANIPULATE THE DOTS ON THE SCREEN.
SO WHEN WE TURN THIS KNOB, IT'LL ACTUALLY MOVE THE IMAGE ON THE TV?
EXACTLY!
LIKE MAGIC.
BUT WHEN I SHOWED THE BOSSES, THEY THOUGHT I WAS NUTS!
YOU WANT PEOPLE TO SIT IN FRONT OF A SCREEN AND PLAY WITH DOTS AND LINES?
I KNOW IT LOOKS BASIC, BUT THIS IS THE FUTURE!
HERE'S $2,500 FOR RESEARCH AND MATERIALS.
BUT THAT'S ALL YOU'RE GETTING.

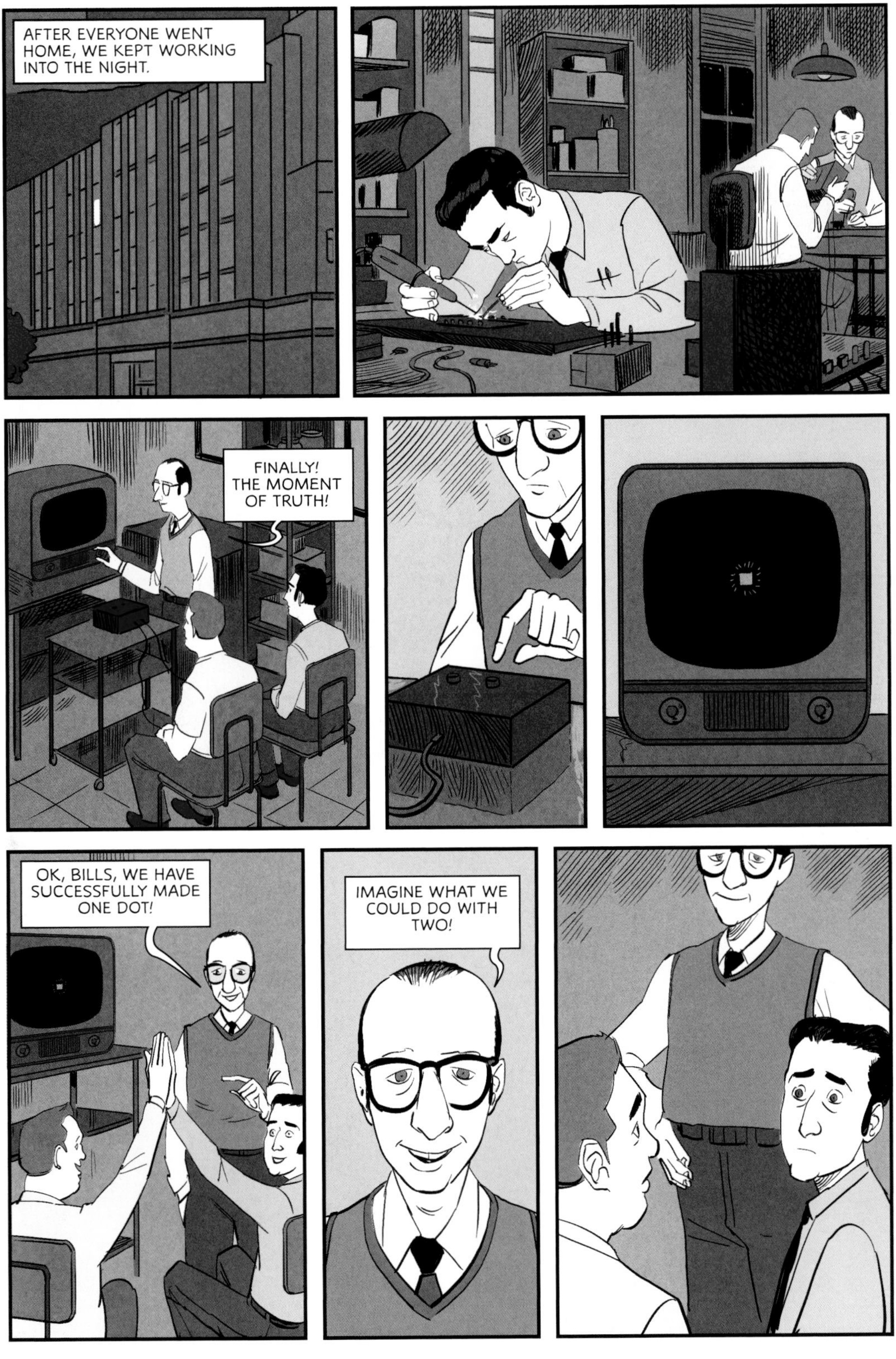
AFTER EVERYONE WENT HOME, WE KEPT WORKING INTO THE NIGHT.
FINALLY! THE MOMENT OF TRUTH!
OK, BILLS, WE HAVE SUCCESSFULLY MADE ONE DOT!
IMAGINE WHAT WE COULD DO WITH TWO!

WITH A LITTLE MORE WORK, WE MANAGED TO CREATE A TYPE OF PRIMITIVE GAME.

HOPE YOU'RE READY!

OH HO HO! I'M GONNA GET YOU, BILL!

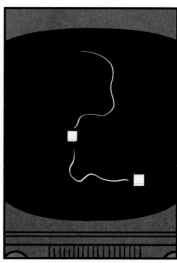

HEY, WATCH IT!

ALMOST GOT YOU!

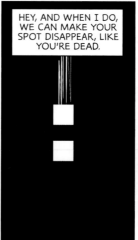

HEY, AND WHEN I DO, WE CAN MAKE YOUR SPOT DISAPPEAR, LIKE YOU'RE DEAD.

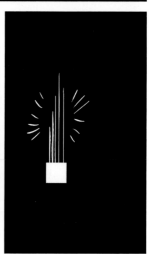

WHAT ELSE CAN WE DO WITH THESE DOTS?

HEY, I GOT IT!

PUT UP ANOTHER SPOT.

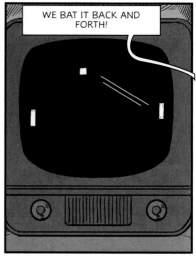

WE BAT IT BACK AND FORTH!

22

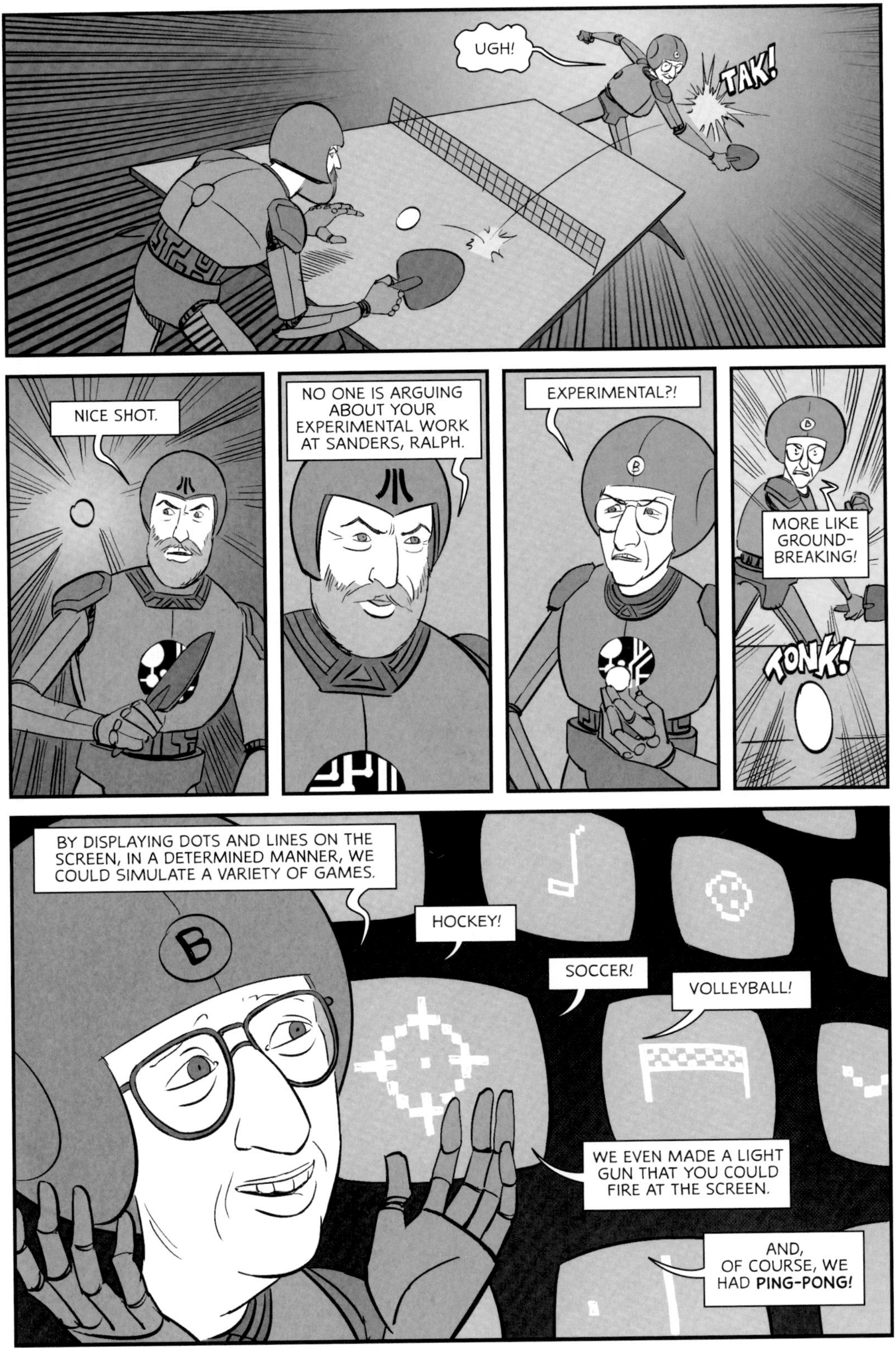
UGH!
TAK!
NICE SHOT.
NO ONE IS ARGUING ABOUT YOUR EXPERIMENTAL WORK AT SANDERS, RALPH.
EXPERIMENTAL?!
MORE LIKE GROUND-BREAKING!
TONK!
BY DISPLAYING DOTS AND LINES ON THE SCREEN, IN A DETERMINED MANNER, WE COULD SIMULATE A VARIETY OF GAMES.
HOCKEY!
SOCCER!
VOLLEYBALL!
WE EVEN MADE A LIGHT GUN THAT YOU COULD FIRE AT THE SCREEN.
AND, OF COURSE, WE HAD **PING-PONG!**

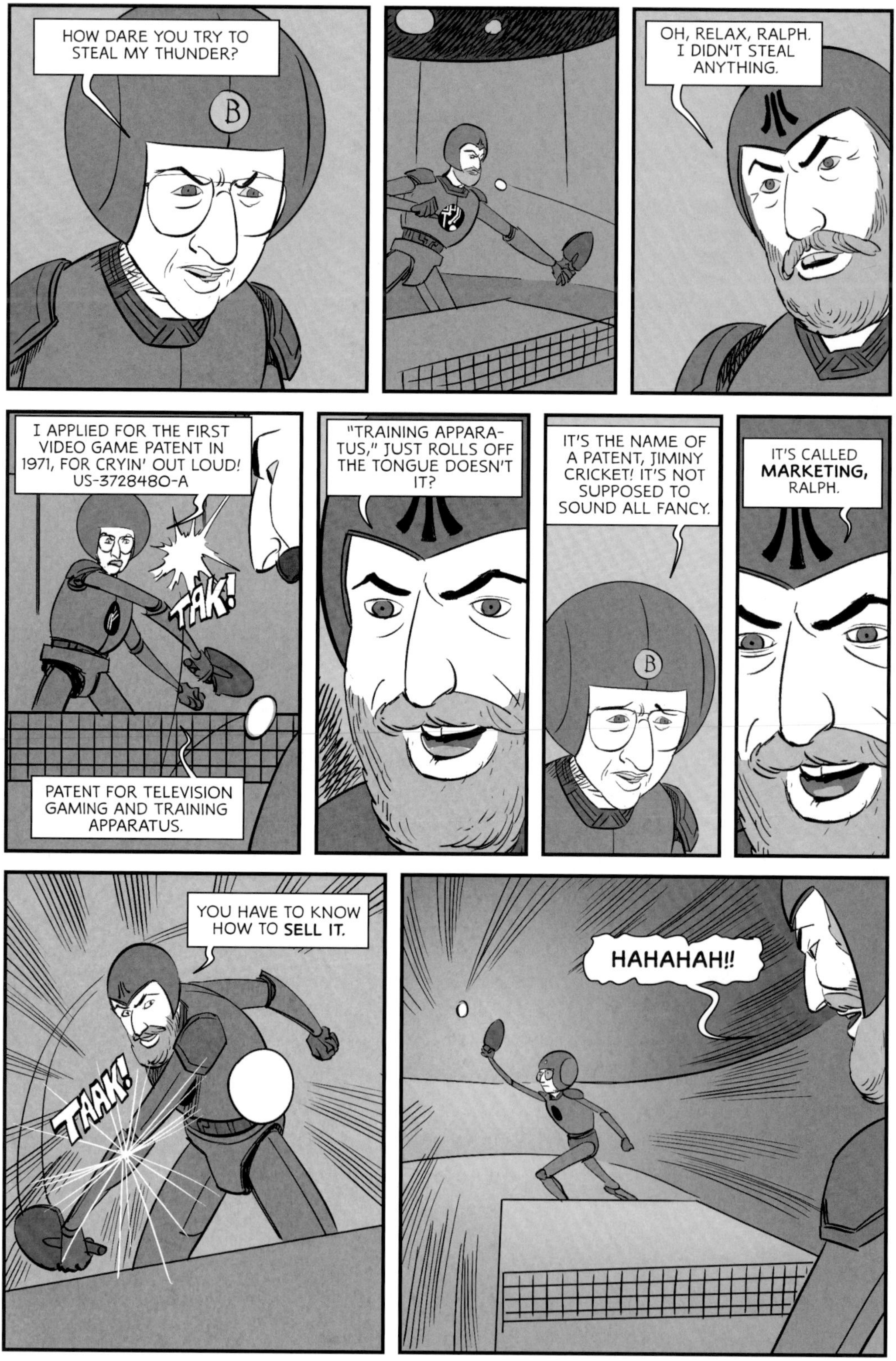
HOW DARE YOU TRY TO STEAL MY THUNDER?
OH, RELAX, RALPH. I DIDN'T STEAL ANYTHING.
I APPLIED FOR THE FIRST VIDEO GAME PATENT IN 1971, FOR CRYIN' OUT LOUD! US-3728480-A
TAK!
PATENT FOR TELEVISION GAMING AND TRAINING APPARATUS.
"TRAINING APPARATUS," JUST ROLLS OFF THE TONGUE DOESN'T IT?
IT'S THE NAME OF A PATENT, JIMINY CRICKET! IT'S NOT SUPPOSED TO SOUND ALL FANCY.
IT'S CALLED **MARKETING,** RALPH.
YOU HAVE TO KNOW HOW TO **SELL IT.**
TAAK!
HAHAHAH!!

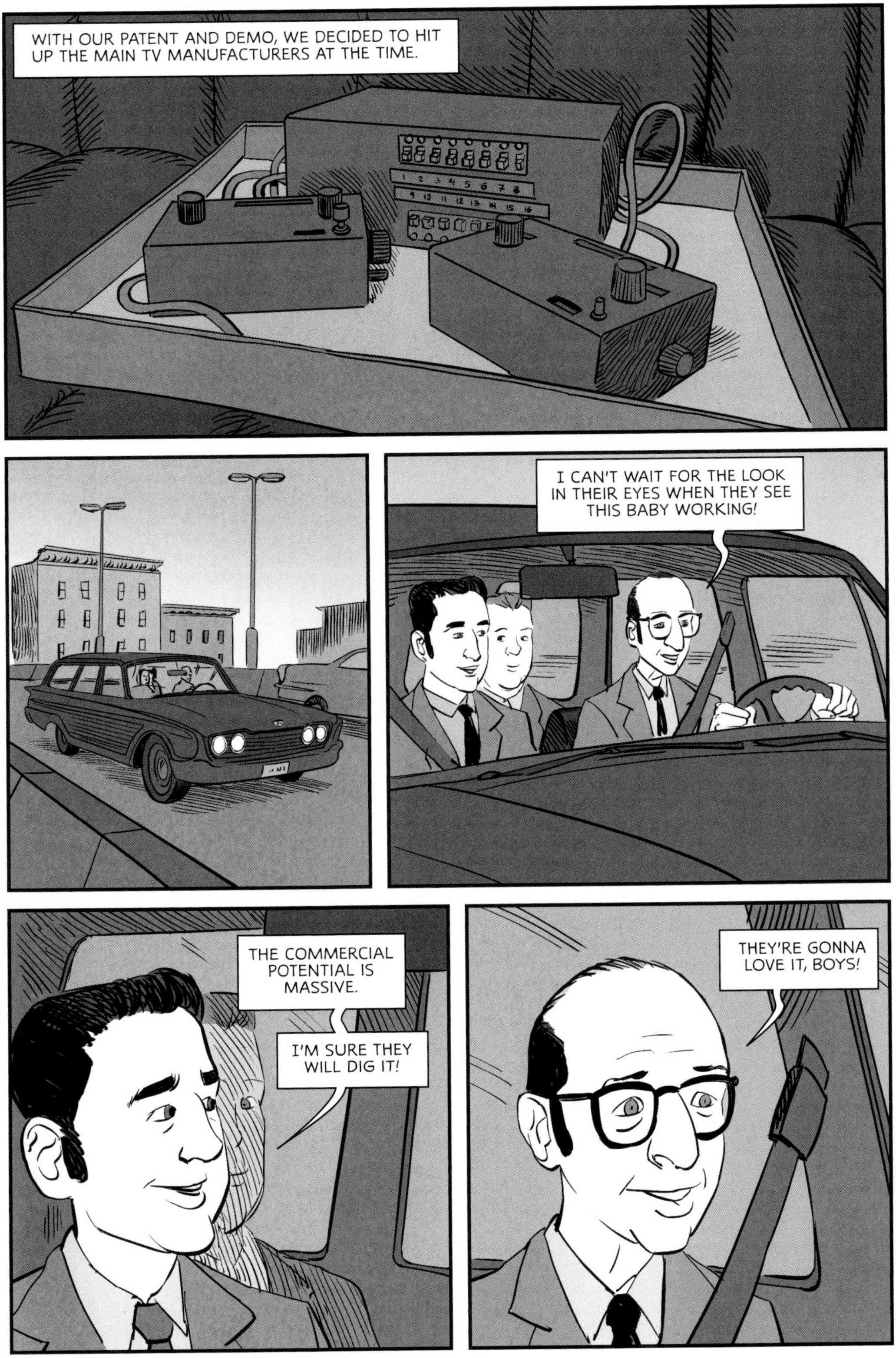
WITH OUR PATENT AND DEMO, WE DECIDED TO HIT UP THE MAIN TV MANUFACTURERS AT THE TIME.
I CAN'T WAIT FOR THE LOOK IN THEIR EYES WHEN THEY SEE THIS BABY WORKING!
THE COMMERCIAL POTENTIAL IS MASSIVE.
I'M SURE THEY WILL DIG IT!
THEY'RE GONNA LOVE IT, BOYS!

GE HEADQUARTERS, BOSTON, MASSACHUSETTS, 1969

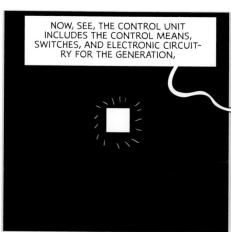
NOW, SEE, THE CONTROL UNIT INCLUDES THE CONTROL MEANS, SWITCHES, AND ELECTRONIC CIRCUITRY FOR THE GENERATION,

MANIPULATION, AND CONTROL OF VIDEO SIGNALS THAT ARE TO BE DISPLAYED ON THE TELEVISION SCREEN.

A GAME. ON A TELEVISION SET?

I KNOW IT SOUNDS CRAZY, BUT--

THIS IS GREAT!

IT IS?

I MEAN, IT IS!

BUT WE COULD NEVER SELL THIS.

THIS IS 1969, MR. BAER, AND PEOPLE WANT TO WATCH SHOWS ON THEIR TVS--LAUGH-IN, GUNSMOKE, THE BRADY BUNCH. THAT'S THE WHOLE POINT!

AND IF PEOPLE WANT GAMES, WELL, GAMES COME IN A BOX.

NOT A TELEVISION SET.

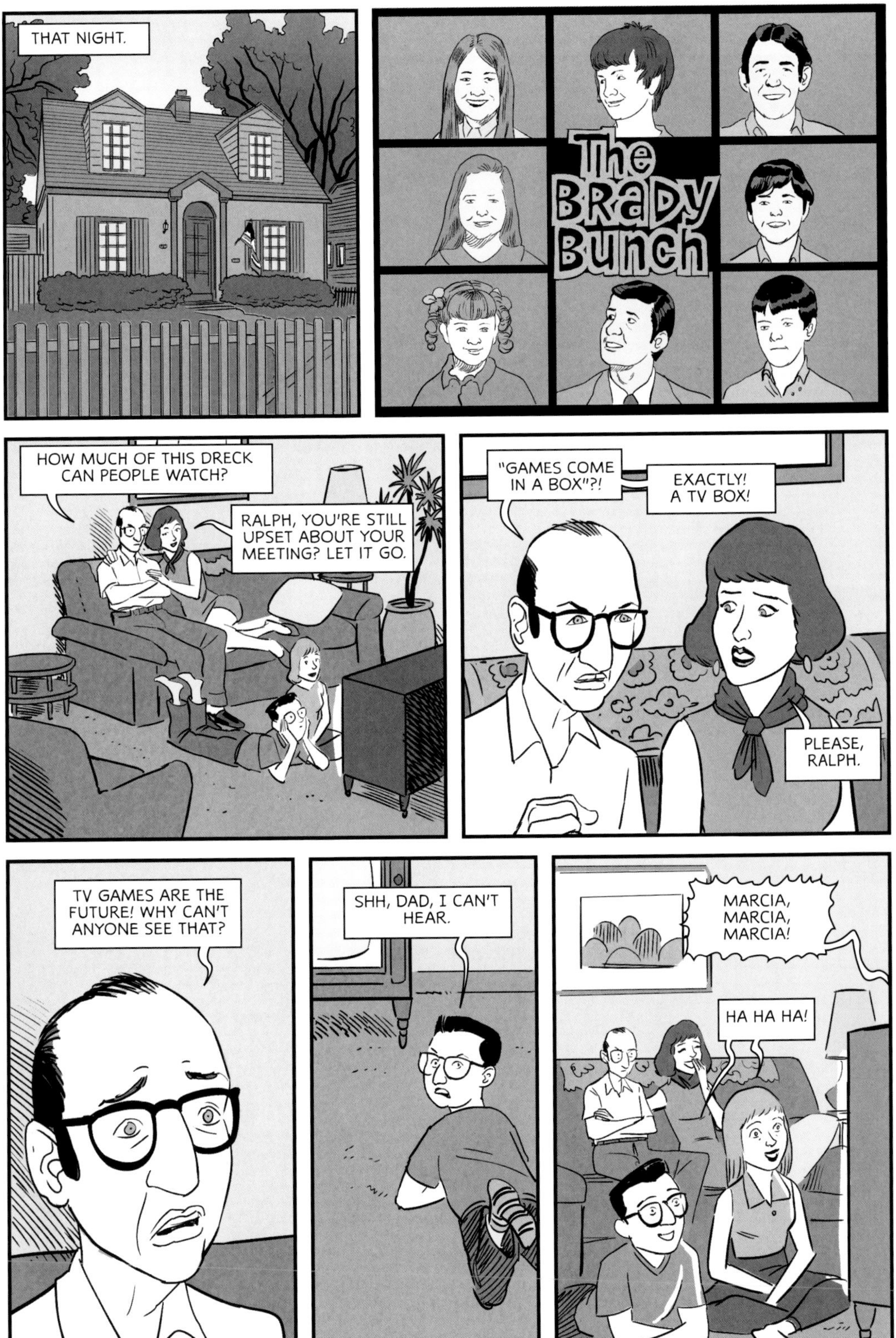
THAT NIGHT.
The Brady Bunch
HOW MUCH OF THIS DRECK CAN PEOPLE WATCH?
RALPH, YOU'RE STILL UPSET ABOUT YOUR MEETING? LET IT GO.
"GAMES COME IN A BOX"?!
EXACTLY! A TV BOX!
PLEASE, RALPH.
TV GAMES ARE THE FUTURE! WHY CAN'T ANYONE SEE THAT?
SHH, DAD, I CAN'T HEAR.
MARCIA, MARCIA, MARCIA!
HA HA HA!

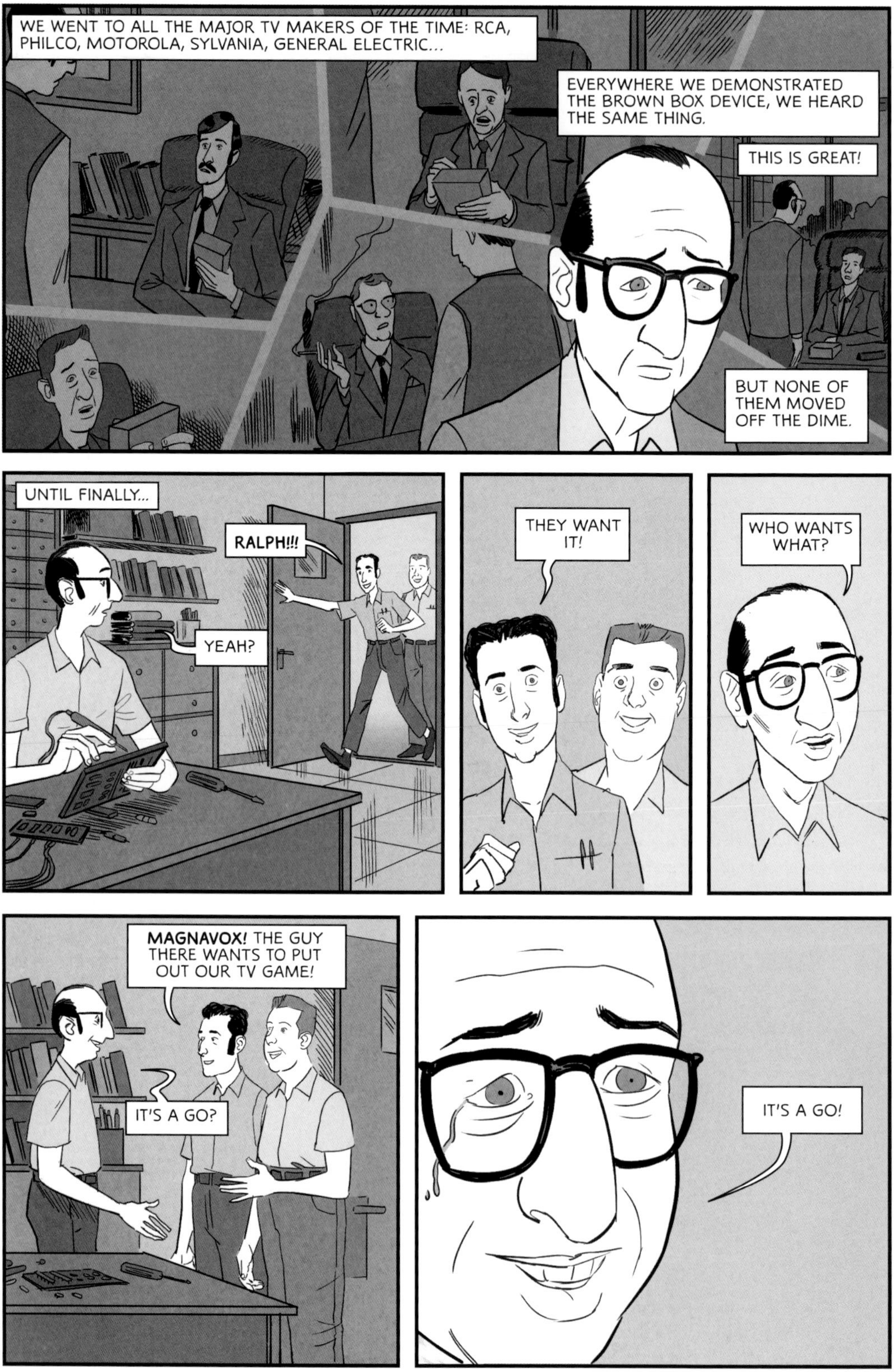
WE WENT TO ALL THE MAJOR TV MAKERS OF THE TIME: RCA, PHILCO, MOTOROLA, SYLVANIA, GENERAL ELECTRIC...
EVERYWHERE WE DEMONSTRATED THE BROWN BOX DEVICE, WE HEARD THE SAME THING.
THIS IS GREAT!
BUT NONE OF THEM MOVED OFF THE DIME.
UNTIL FINALLY...
RALPH!!!
YEAH?
THEY WANT IT!
WHO WANTS WHAT?
MAGNAVOX! THE GUY THERE WANTS TO PUT OUT OUR TV GAME!
IT'S A GO?
IT'S A GO!

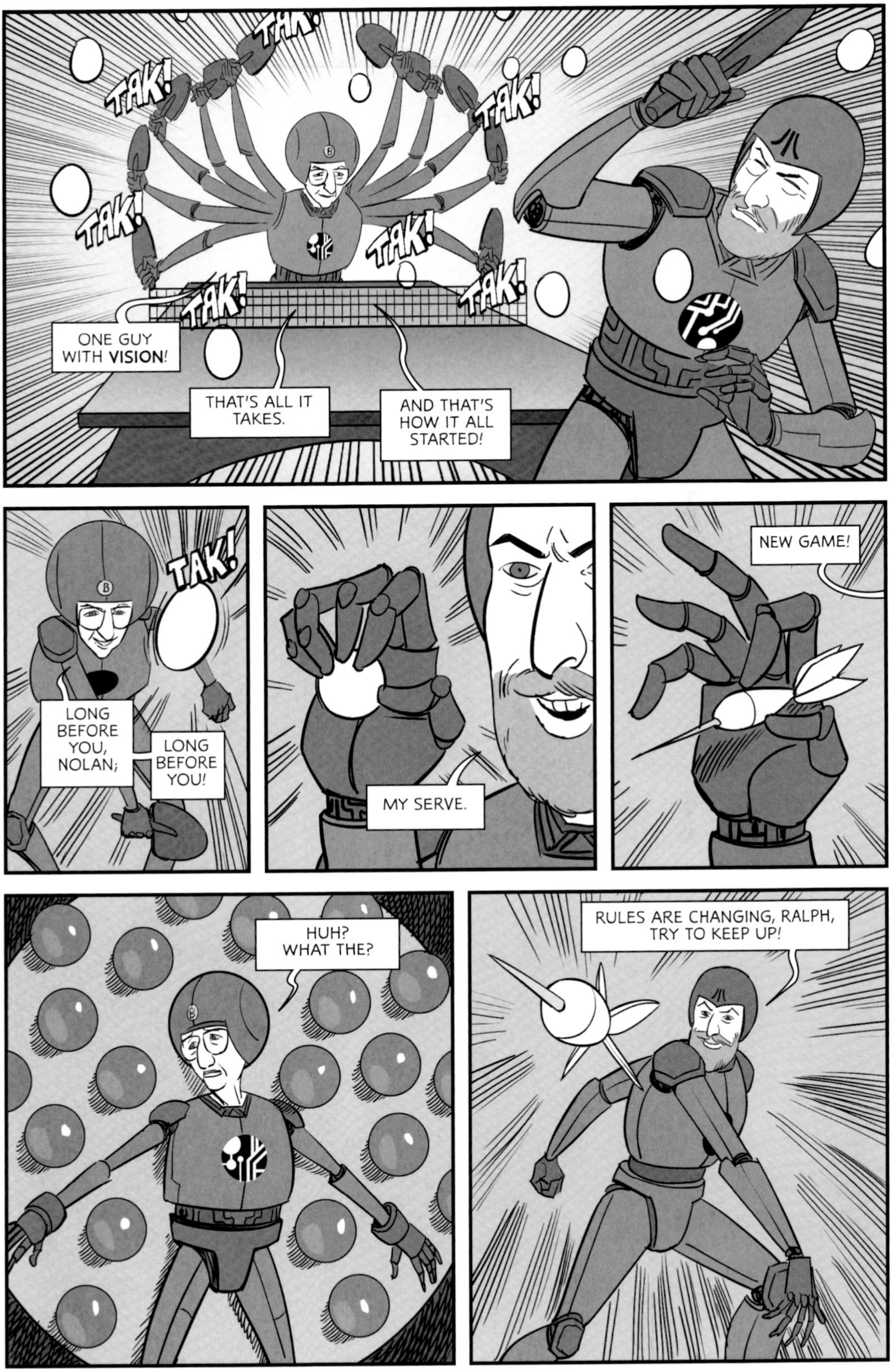
TAK!
TAK!
TAK!
TAK!
TAK!
TAK!
TAK!
ONE GUY WITH **VISION**!
THAT'S ALL IT TAKES.
AND THAT'S HOW IT ALL STARTED!
TAK!
LONG BEFORE YOU, NOLAN;
LONG BEFORE YOU!
MY SERVE.
NEW GAME!
HUH? WHAT THE?
RULES ARE CHANGING, RALPH, TRY TO KEEP UP!

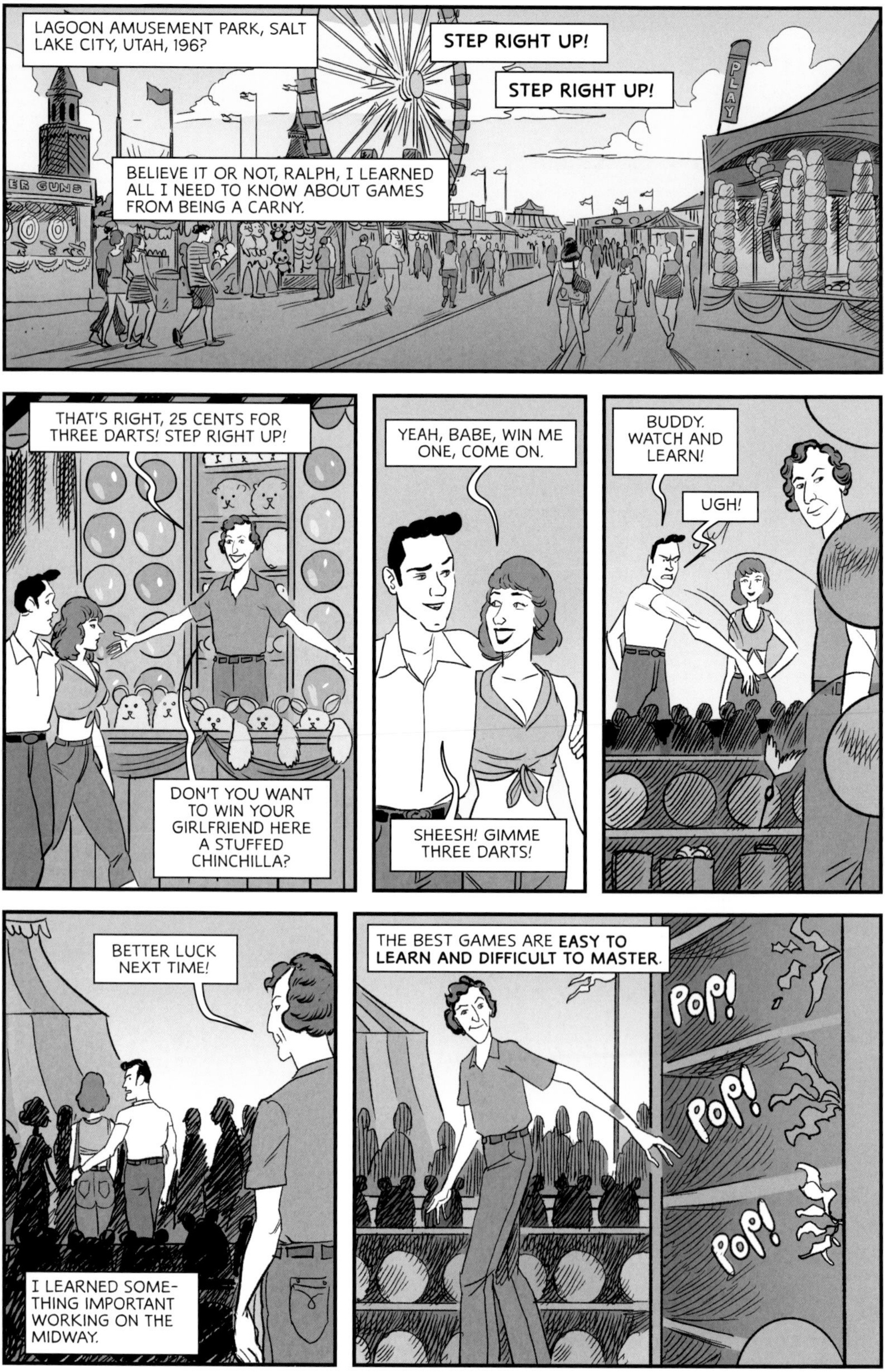
LAGOON AMUSEMENT PARK, SALT LAKE CITY, UTAH, 196?
STEP RIGHT UP!
STEP RIGHT UP!
PLAY
BELIEVE IT OR NOT, RALPH, I LEARNED ALL I NEED TO KNOW ABOUT GAMES FROM BEING A CARNY.
THAT'S RIGHT, 25 CENTS FOR THREE DARTS! STEP RIGHT UP!
DON'T YOU WANT TO WIN YOUR GIRLFRIEND HERE A STUFFED CHINCHILLA?
YEAH, BABE, WIN ME ONE, COME ON.
SHEESH! GIMME THREE DARTS!
BUDDY. WATCH AND LEARN!
UGH!
BETTER LUCK NEXT TIME!
I LEARNED SOMETHING IMPORTANT WORKING ON THE MIDWAY.
THE BEST GAMES ARE **EASY TO LEARN AND DIFFICULT TO MASTER**.
POP!
POP!
POP!

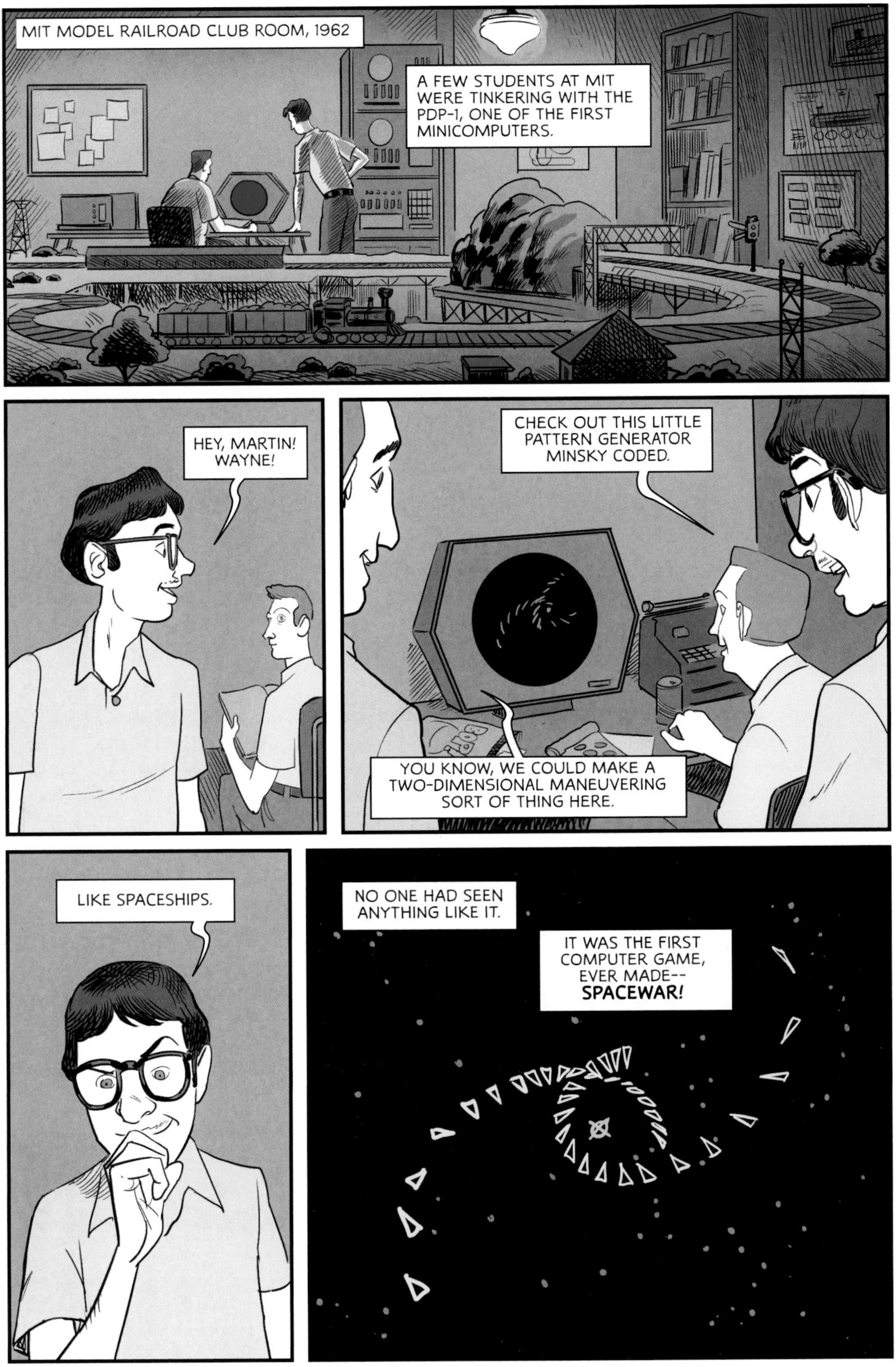
MIT MODEL RAILROAD CLUB ROOM, 1962
A FEW STUDENTS AT MIT WERE TINKERING WITH THE PDP-1, ONE OF THE FIRST MINICOMPUTERS.
HEY, MARTIN! WAYNE!
CHECK OUT THIS LITTLE PATTERN GENERATOR MINSKY CODED.
YOU KNOW, WE COULD MAKE A TWO-DIMENSIONAL MANEUVERING SORT OF THING HERE.
LIKE SPACESHIPS.
NO ONE HAD SEEN ANYTHING LIKE IT.
IT WAS THE FIRST COMPUTER GAME, EVER MADE-- **SPACEWAR!**

UNIVERSITY OF UTAH COMPUTER LAB

SO I JUST TORPEDO THIS SHIP?

YEAH, NOLAN!

BUT YOU GOTTA THRUST AWAY FROM THE GRAVITATIONAL FIELD, OR YOU'LL--

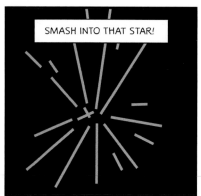

SMASH INTO THAT STAR!

OH, MAN!

THIS IS AMAZING

IF I HAD THIS IN MY AMUSEMENT PARK, I'D MAKE A LOT OF MONEY.

WHERE'D YOU BUY THIS?

I DIDN'T!

YOU STOLE IT?

NO! THE GUYS WHO MADE IT SHARED THEIR CODE, SO NOW WE CAN ALL MAKE OUR OWN VERSIONS OF THE GAME.

NO KIDDING!

HOW CONSIDERATE.

32

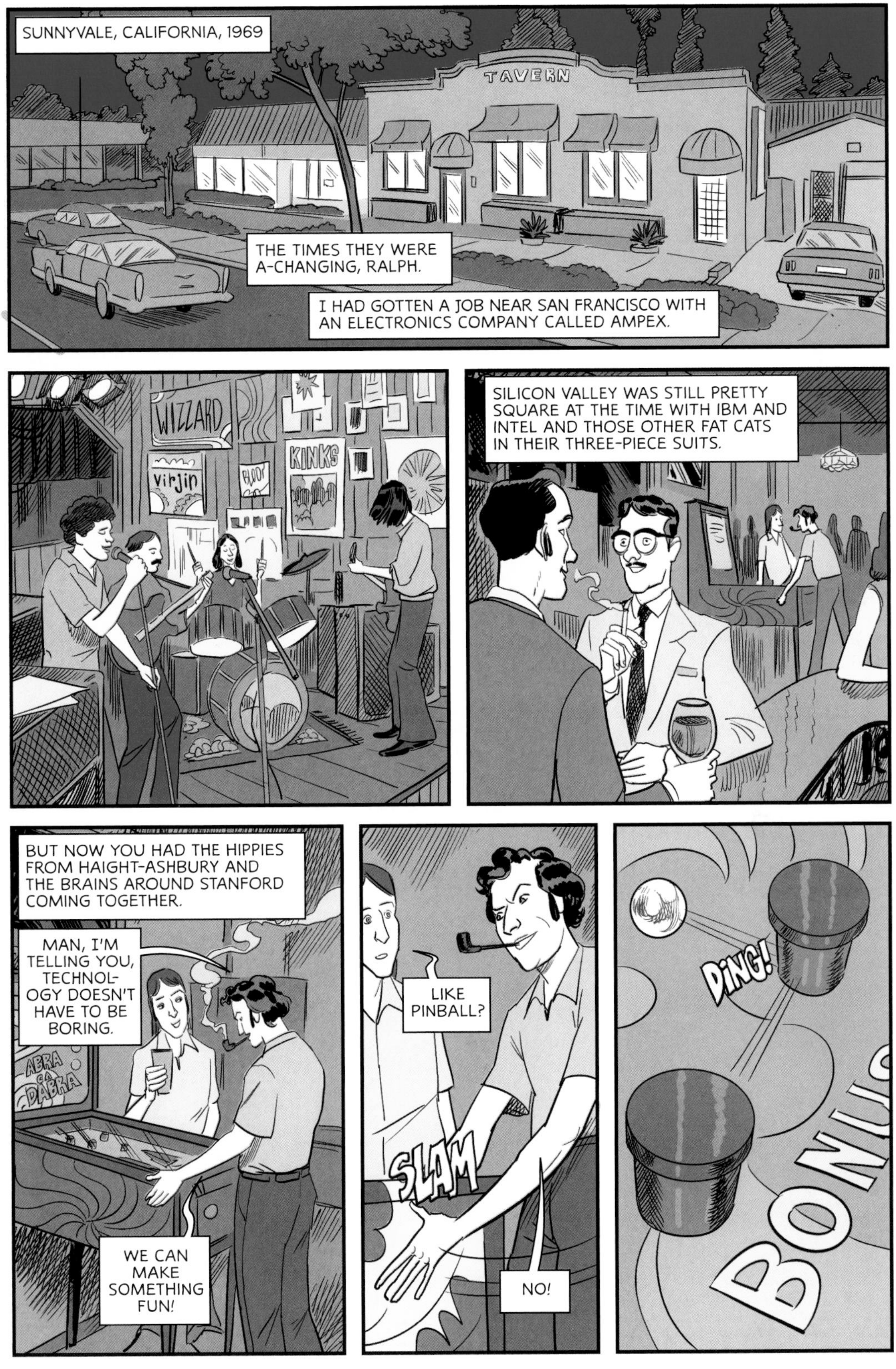

SUNNYVALE, CALIFORNIA, 1969
TAVERN
THE TIMES THEY WERE A-CHANGING, RALPH.
I HAD GOTTEN A JOB NEAR SAN FRANCISCO WITH AN ELECTRONICS COMPANY CALLED AMPEX.
WIZZARD
KINKS
virjin
SILICON VALLEY WAS STILL PRETTY SQUARE AT THE TIME WITH IBM AND INTEL AND THOSE OTHER FAT CATS IN THEIR THREE-PIECE SUITS.
BUT NOW YOU HAD THE HIPPIES FROM HAIGHT-ASHBURY AND THE BRAINS AROUND STANFORD COMING TOGETHER.
MAN, I'M TELLING YOU, TECHNOL-OGY DOESN'T HAVE TO BE BORING.
ABRA CA DABRA
WE CAN MAKE SOMETHING FUN!
LIKE PINBALL?
SLAM
NO!
DING!

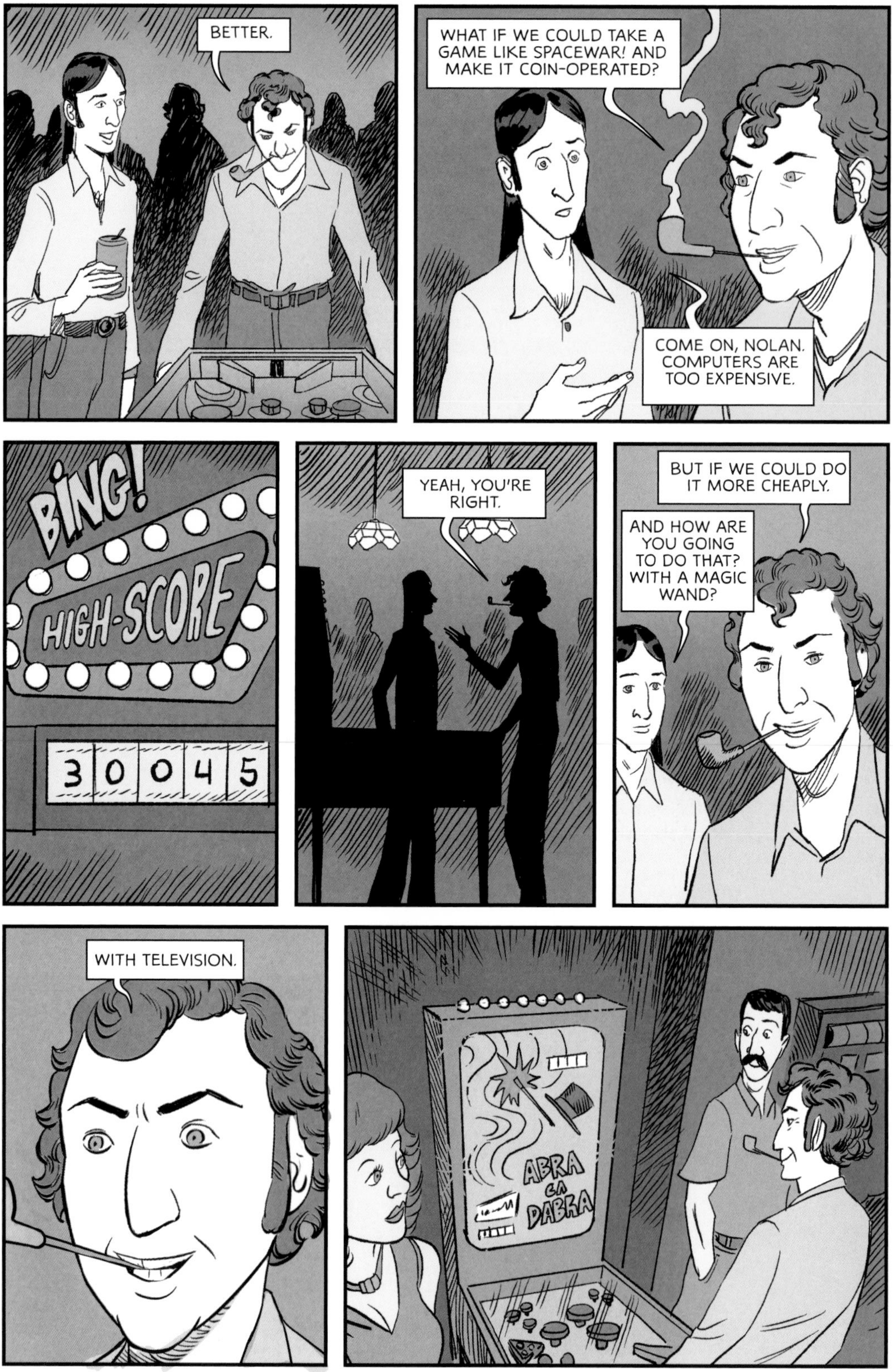
BETTER.
WHAT IF WE COULD TAKE A GAME LIKE SPACEWAR! AND MAKE IT COIN-OPERATED?
COME ON, NOLAN. COMPUTERS ARE TOO EXPENSIVE.
BING!
HIGH-SCORE
30045
YEAH, YOU'RE RIGHT.
BUT IF WE COULD DO IT MORE CHEAPLY.
AND HOW ARE YOU GOING TO DO THAT? WITH A MAGIC WAND?
WITH TELEVISION.
ABRA CA DABRA

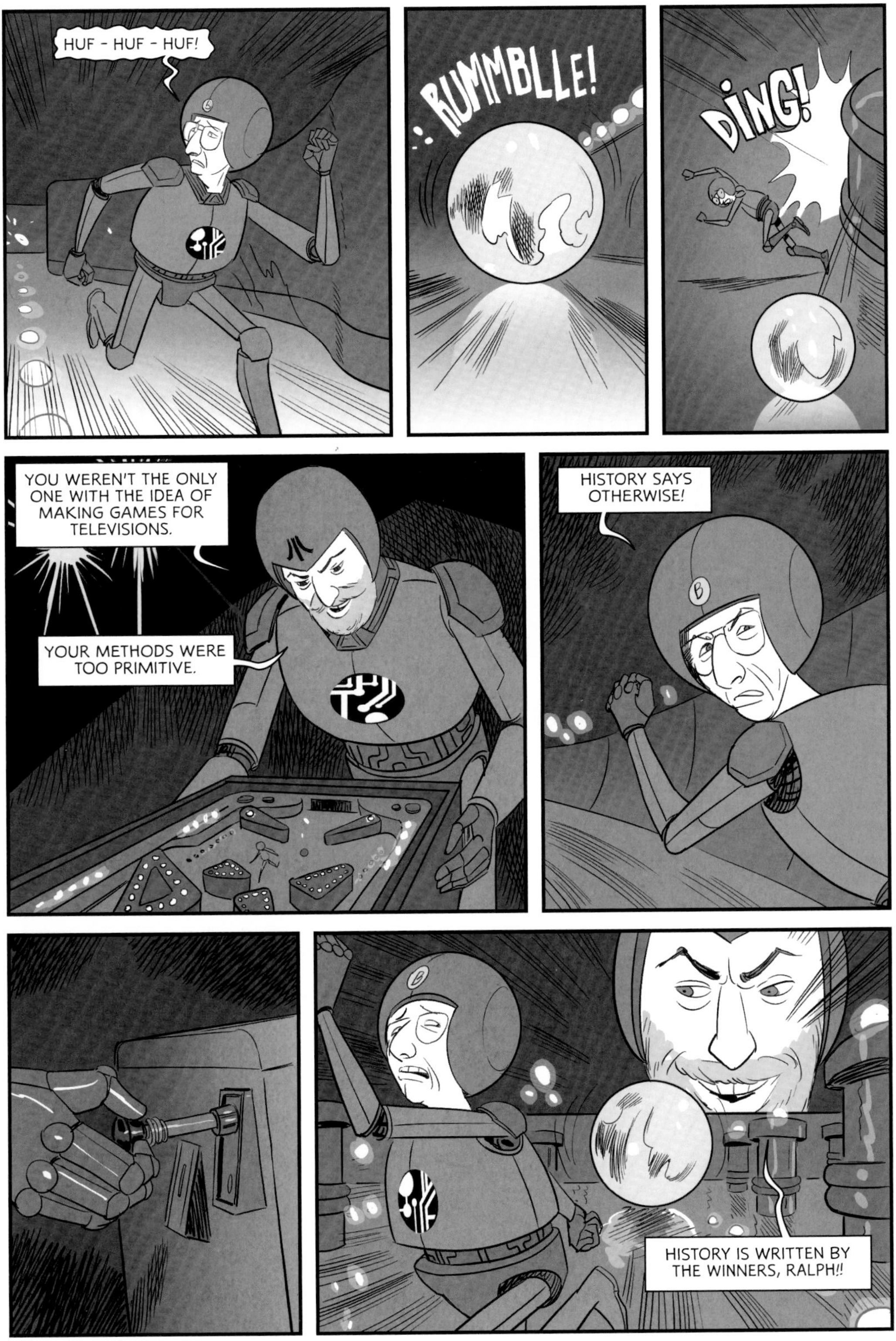
HUF - HUF - HUF!
RUMMBLLE!
DING!
YOU WEREN'T THE ONLY ONE WITH THE IDEA OF MAKING GAMES FOR TELEVISIONS.
YOUR METHODS WERE TOO PRIMITIVE.
HISTORY SAYS OTHERWISE!
HISTORY IS WRITTEN BY THE WINNERS, RALPH!!

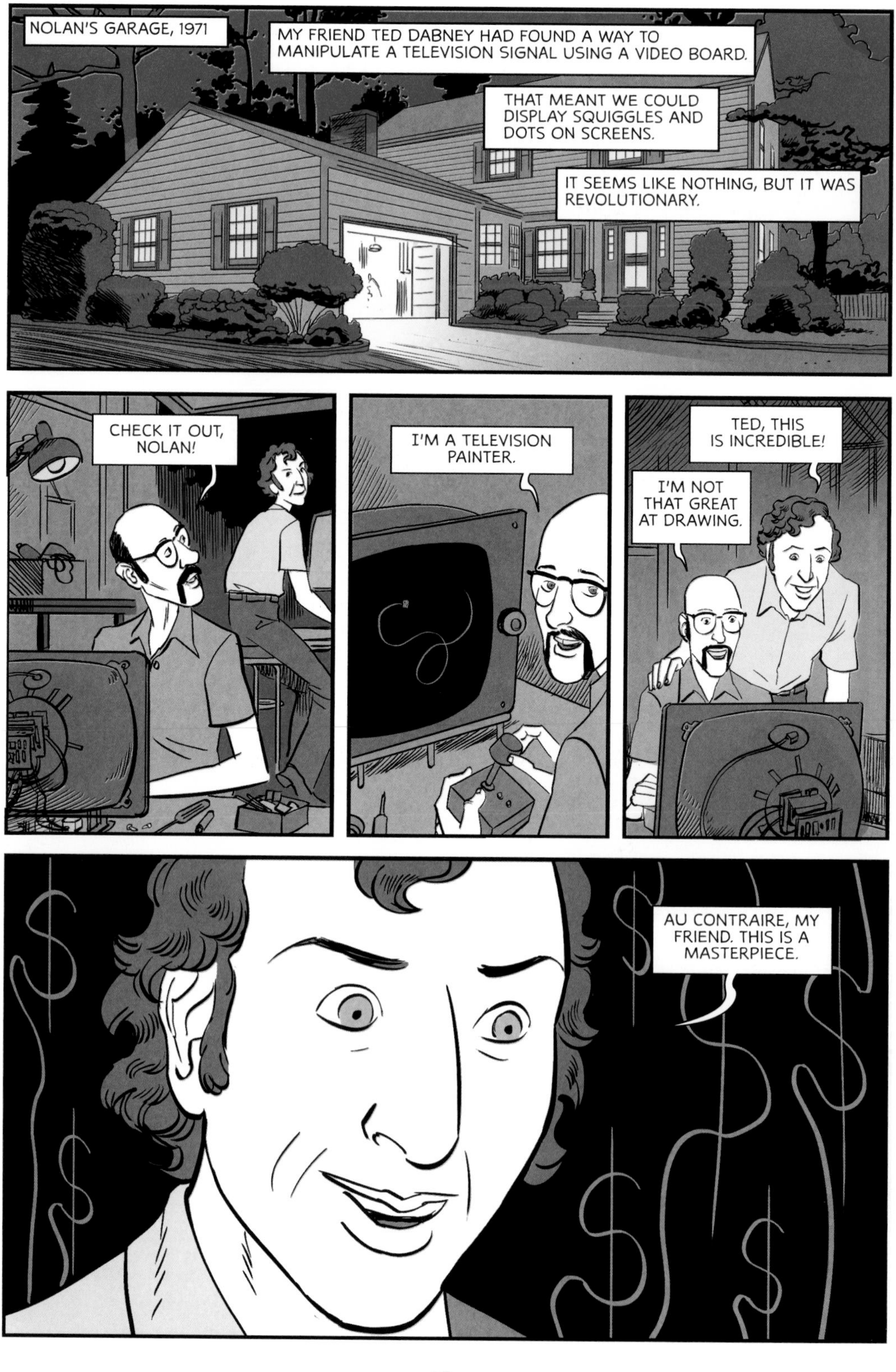
NOLAN'S GARAGE, 1971
MY FRIEND TED DABNEY HAD FOUND A WAY TO MANIPULATE A TELEVISION SIGNAL USING A VIDEO BOARD.
THAT MEANT WE COULD DISPLAY SQUIGGLES AND DOTS ON SCREENS.
IT SEEMS LIKE NOTHING, BUT IT WAS REVOLUTIONARY.
CHECK IT OUT, NOLAN!
I'M A TELEVISION PAINTER.
TED, THIS IS INCREDIBLE!
I'M NOT THAT GREAT AT DRAWING.
AU CONTRAIRE, MY FRIEND. THIS IS A MASTERPIECE.

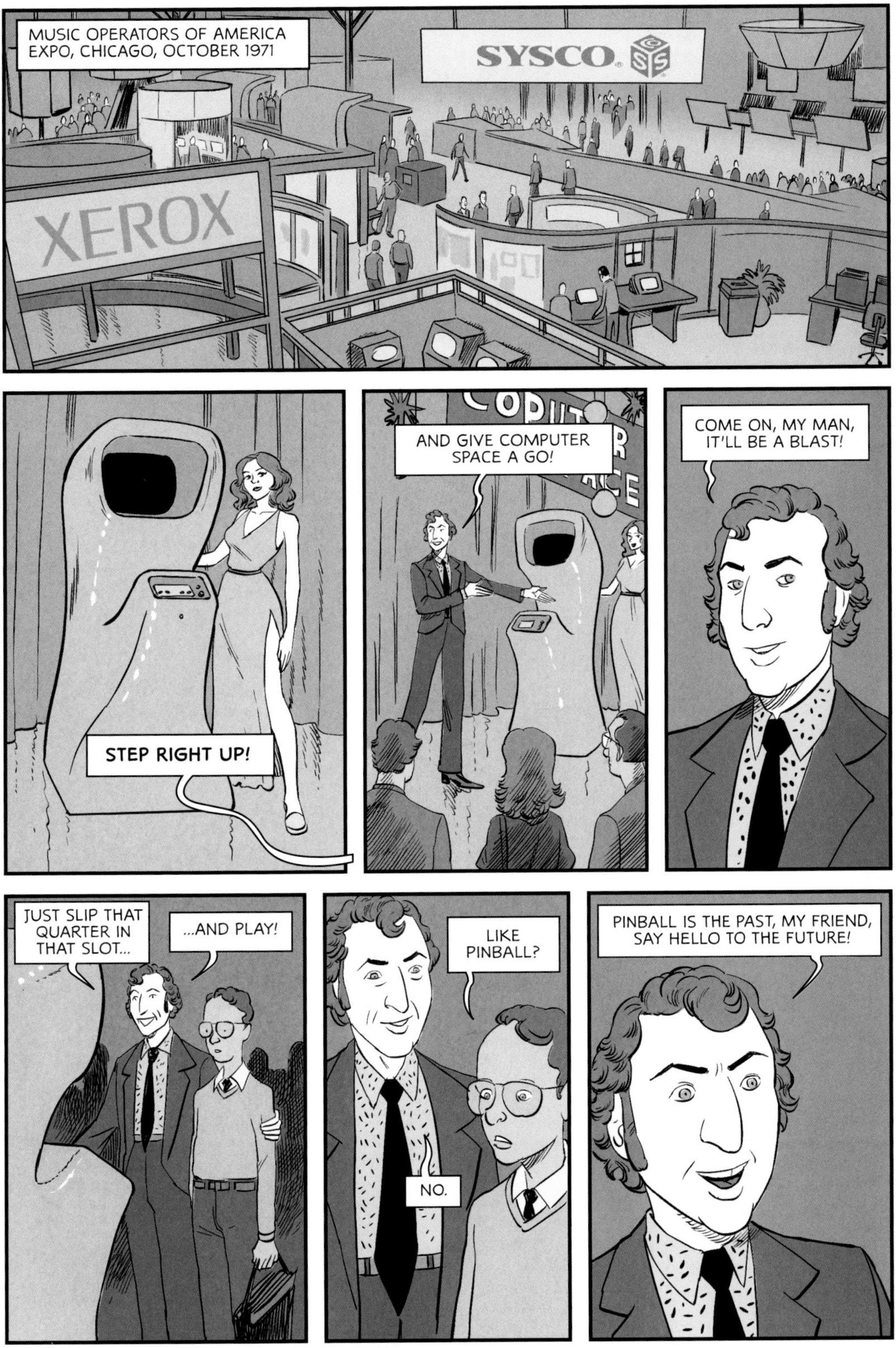
MUSIC OPERATORS OF AMERICA EXPO, CHICAGO, OCTOBER 1971
SYSCO
XEROX
STEP RIGHT UP!
AND GIVE COMPUTER SPACE A GO!
COME ON, MY MAN, IT'LL BE A BLAST!
JUST SLIP THAT QUARTER IN THAT SLOT...
...AND PLAY!
LIKE PINBALL?
NO.
PINBALL IS THE PAST, MY FRIEND, SAY HELLO TO THE FUTURE!

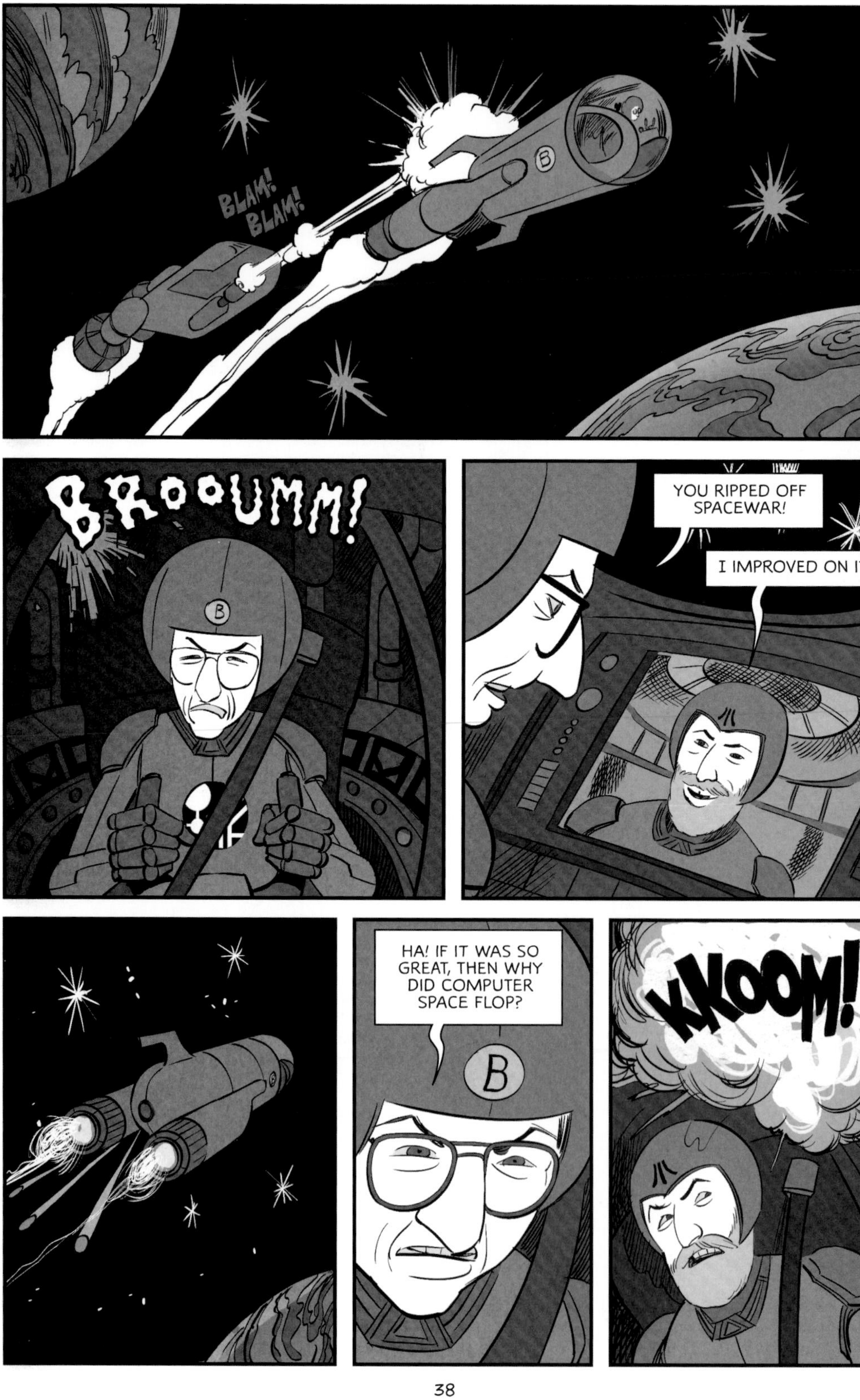
BLAM! BLAM!
BROOUMM!
YOU RIPPED OFF SPACEWAR!
I IMPROVED ON IT.
HA! IF IT WAS SO GREAT, THEN WHY DID COMPUTER SPACE FLOP?
KKOOM!

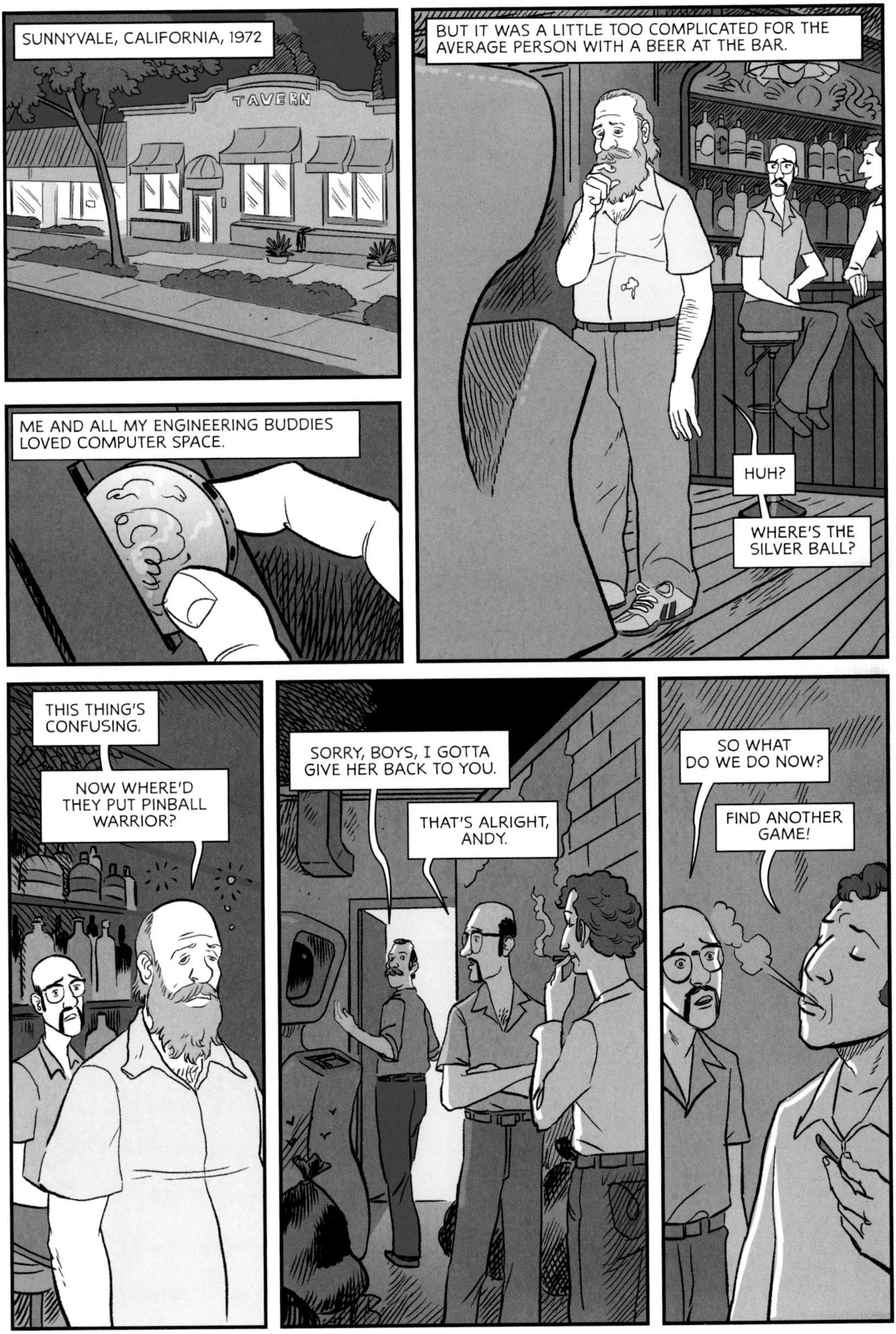
SUNNYVALE, CALIFORNIA, 1972
TAVERN
BUT IT WAS A LITTLE TOO COMPLICATED FOR THE AVERAGE PERSON WITH A BEER AT THE BAR.
ME AND ALL MY ENGINEERING BUDDIES LOVED COMPUTER SPACE.
HUH?
WHERE'S THE SILVER BALL?
THIS THING'S CONFUSING.
NOW WHERE'D THEY PUT PINBALL WARRIOR?
SORRY, BOYS, I GOTTA GIVE HER BACK TO YOU.
THAT'S ALRIGHT, ANDY.
SO WHAT DO WE DO NOW?
FIND ANOTHER GAME!

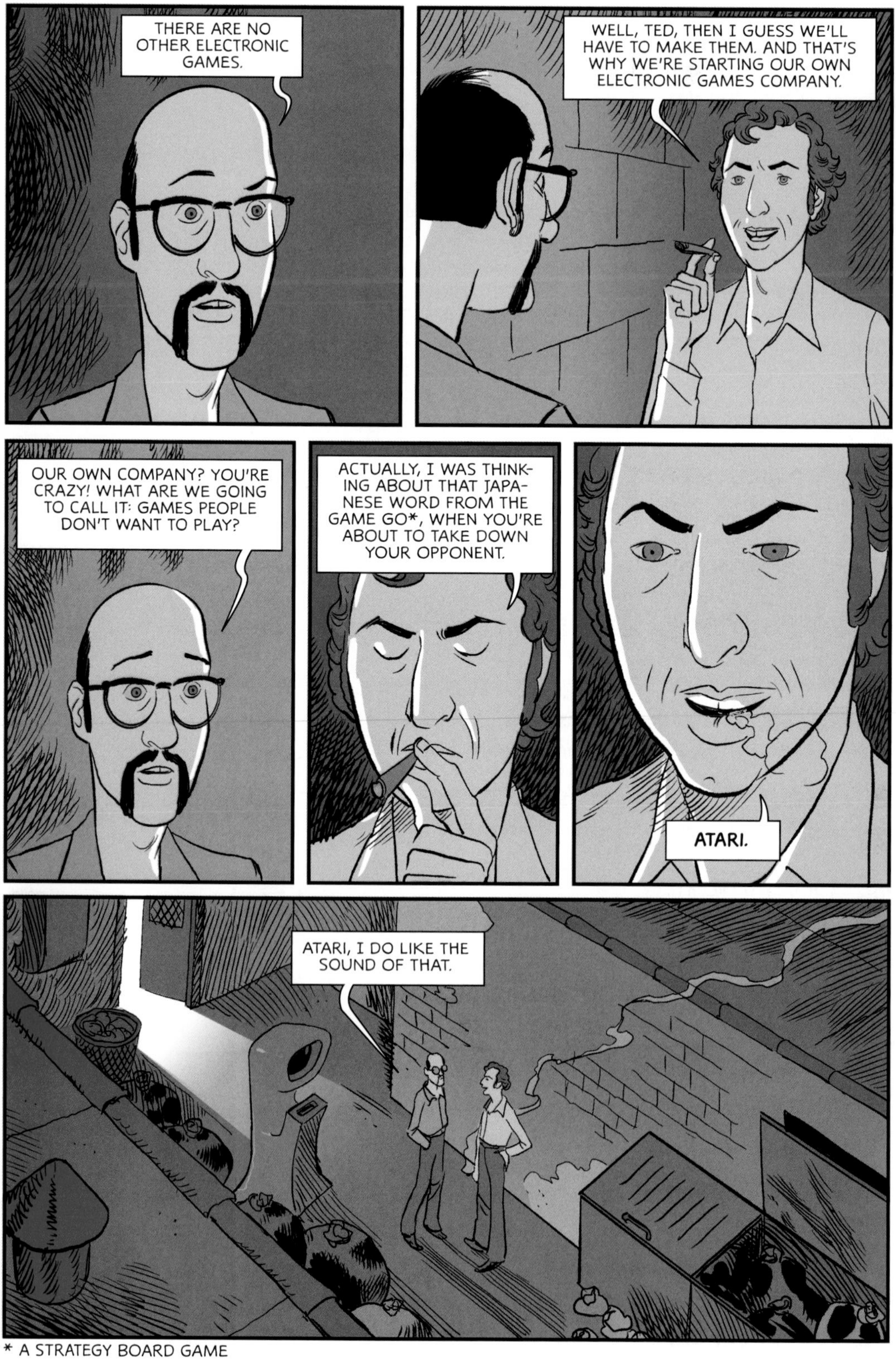
THERE ARE NO OTHER ELECTRONIC GAMES.
WELL, TED, THEN I GUESS WE'LL HAVE TO MAKE THEM. AND THAT'S WHY WE'RE STARTING OUR OWN ELECTRONIC GAMES COMPANY.
OUR OWN COMPANY? YOU'RE CRAZY! WHAT ARE WE GOING TO CALL IT: GAMES PEOPLE DON'T WANT TO PLAY?
ACTUALLY, I WAS THINKING ABOUT THAT JAPANESE WORD FROM THE GAME GO*, WHEN YOU'RE ABOUT TO TAKE DOWN YOUR OPPONENT.
ATARI.
ATARI, I DO LIKE THE SOUND OF THAT.

* A STRATEGY BOARD GAME

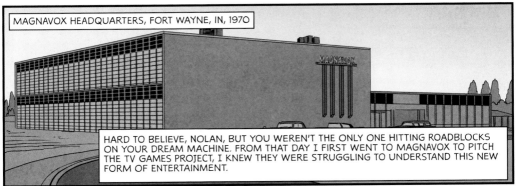

MAGNAVOX HEADQUARTERS, FORT WAYNE, IN, 1970

HARD TO BELIEVE, NOLAN, BUT YOU WEREN'T THE ONLY ONE HITTING ROADBLOCKS ON YOUR DREAM MACHINE. FROM THAT DAY I FIRST WENT TO MAGNAVOX TO PITCH THE TV GAMES PROJECT, I KNEW THEY WERE STRUGGLING TO UNDERSTAND THIS NEW FORM OF ENTERTAINMENT.

SO IF YOU LOOK AT OUR OVERALL SCHEMATIC DIAGRAM FROM THE BROWN BOX, YOU'LL SEE WE UTILIZE THE SYNCH SIGNAL GENERATORS,

THE SECONDARY FLIP-FLOP CIRCUITS, AND THE SPOT GENERATOR CIRCUIT--

I THINK WE CAN TAKE IT FROM HERE, MR. BAER.

VERY WELL! THE BALL IS IN YOUR COURT NOW.

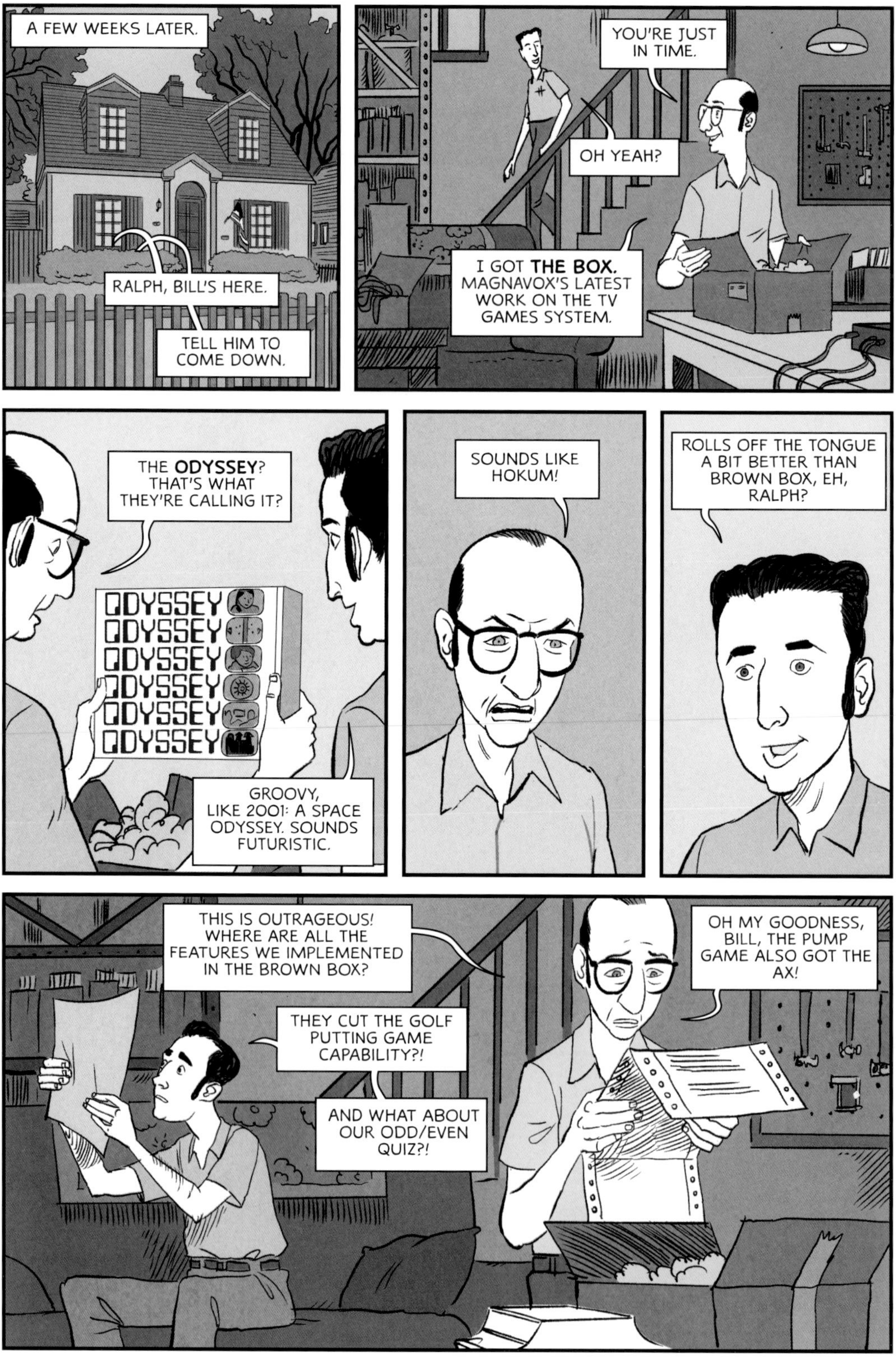
A FEW WEEKS LATER.
RALPH, BILL'S HERE.
TELL HIM TO COME DOWN.
YOU'RE JUST IN TIME.
OH YEAH?
I GOT **THE BOX.** MAGNAVOX'S LATEST WORK ON THE TV GAMES SYSTEM.
THE **ODYSSEY**? THAT'S WHAT THEY'RE CALLING IT?
ODYSSEY
GROOVY, LIKE 2001: A SPACE ODYSSEY. SOUNDS FUTURISTIC.
SOUNDS LIKE HOKUM!
ROLLS OFF THE TONGUE A BIT BETTER THAN BROWN BOX, EH, RALPH?
THIS IS OUTRAGEOUS! WHERE ARE ALL THE FEATURES WE IMPLEMENTED IN THE BROWN BOX?
THEY CUT THE GOLF PUTTING GAME CAPABILITY?!
AND WHAT ABOUT OUR ODD/EVEN QUIZ?!
OH MY GOODNESS, BILL, THE PUMP GAME ALSO GOT THE AX!

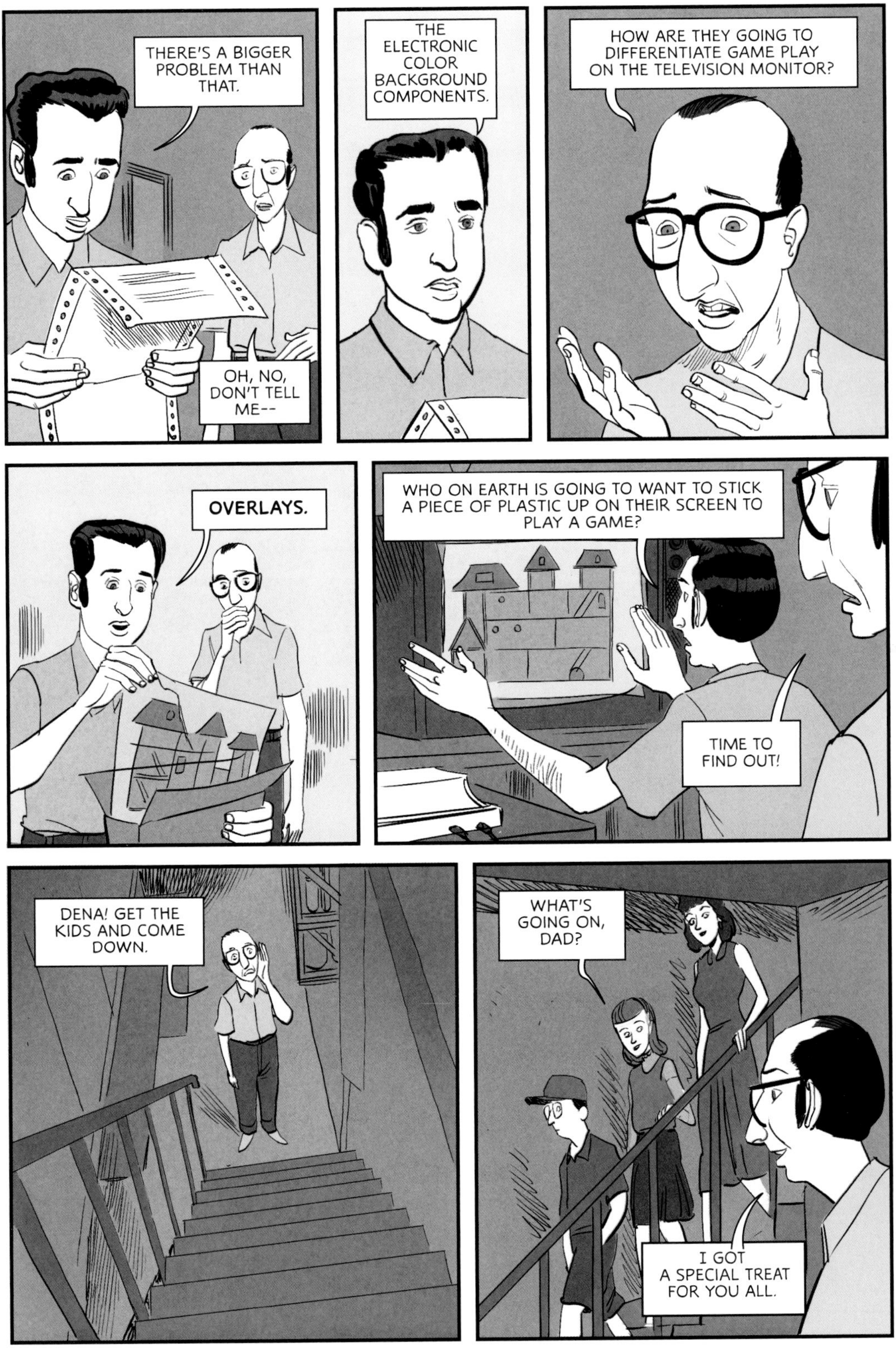
THERE'S A BIGGER PROBLEM THAN THAT.
OH, NO, DON'T TELL ME--
THE ELECTRONIC COLOR BACKGROUND COMPONENTS.
HOW ARE THEY GOING TO DIFFERENTIATE GAME PLAY ON THE TELEVISION MONITOR?
OVERLAYS.
WHO ON EARTH IS GOING TO WANT TO STICK A PIECE OF PLASTIC UP ON THEIR SCREEN TO PLAY A GAME?
TIME TO FIND OUT!
DENA! GET THE KIDS AND COME DOWN.
WHAT'S GOING ON, DAD?
I GOT A SPECIAL TREAT FOR YOU ALL.

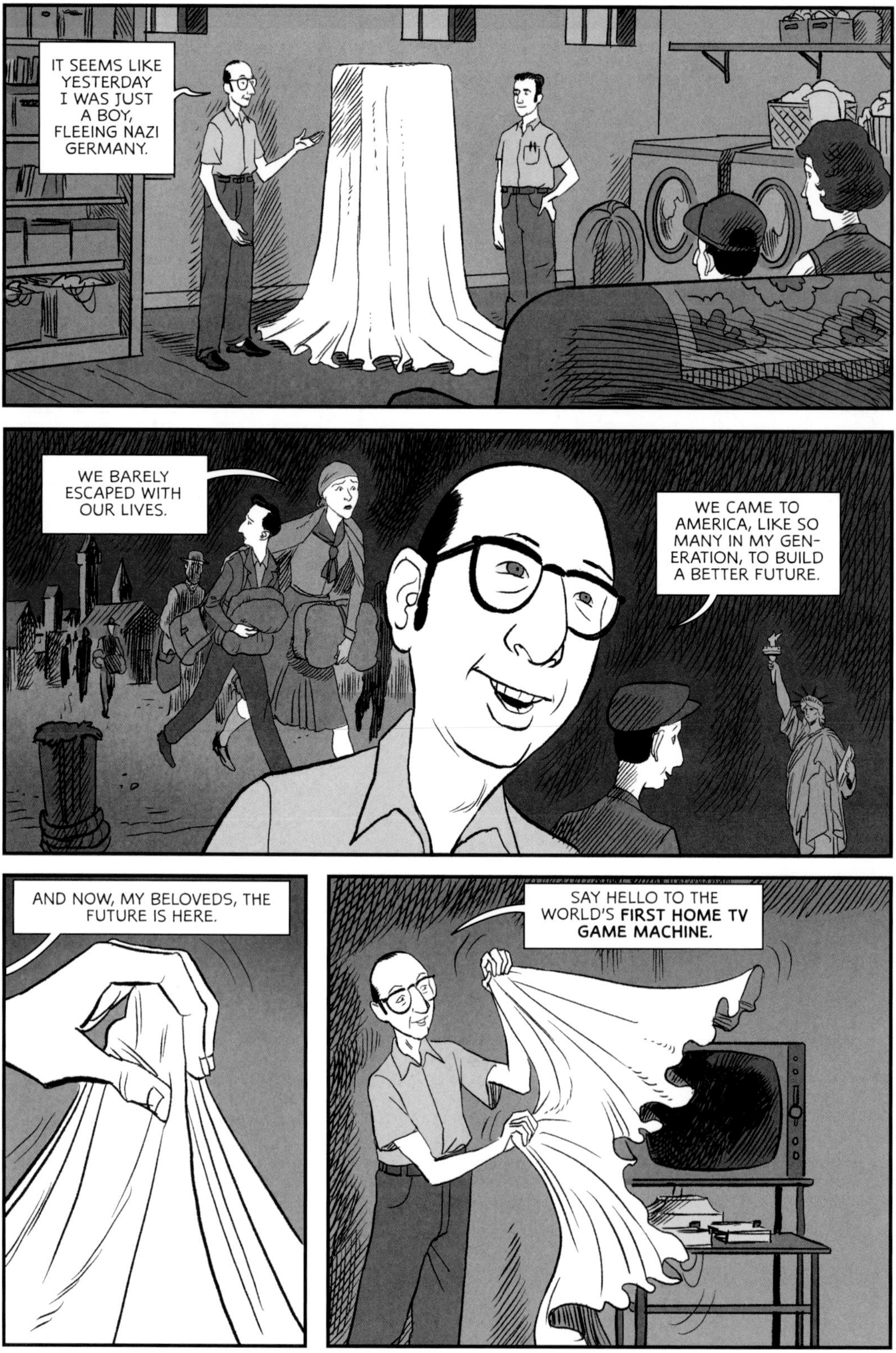
IT SEEMS LIKE YESTERDAY I WAS JUST A BOY, FLEEING NAZI GERMANY.
WE BARELY ESCAPED WITH OUR LIVES.
WE CAME TO AMERICA, LIKE SO MANY IN MY GENERATION, TO BUILD A BETTER FUTURE.
AND NOW, MY BELOVEDS, THE FUTURE IS HERE.
SAY HELLO TO THE WORLD'S FIRST HOME TV GAME MACHINE.

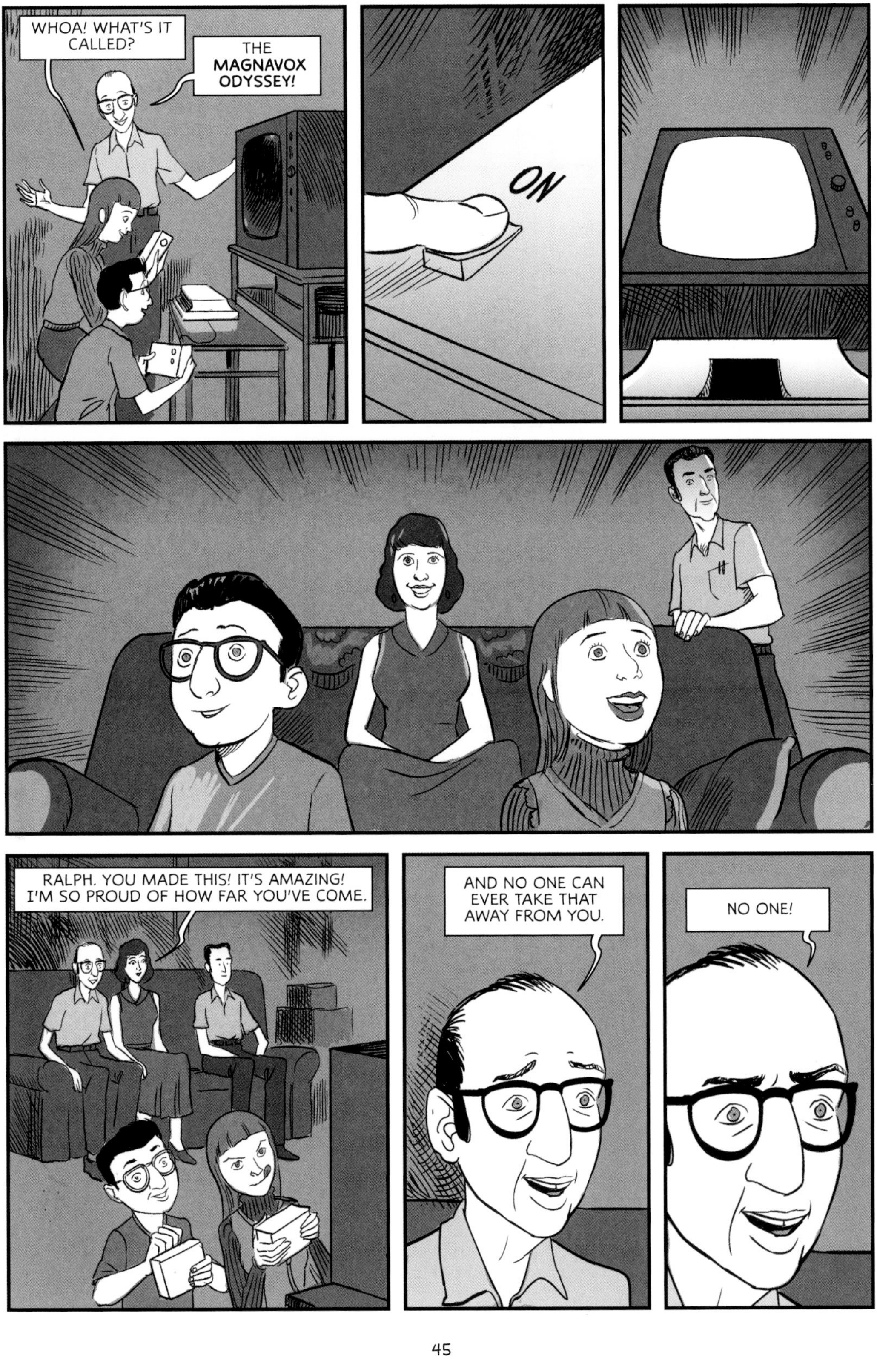
WHOA! WHAT'S IT CALLED?
THE **MAGNAVOX ODYSSEY!**
ON
RALPH. YOU MADE THIS! IT'S AMAZING! I'M SO PROUD OF HOW FAR YOU'VE COME.
AND NO ONE CAN EVER TAKE THAT AWAY FROM YOU.
NO ONE!

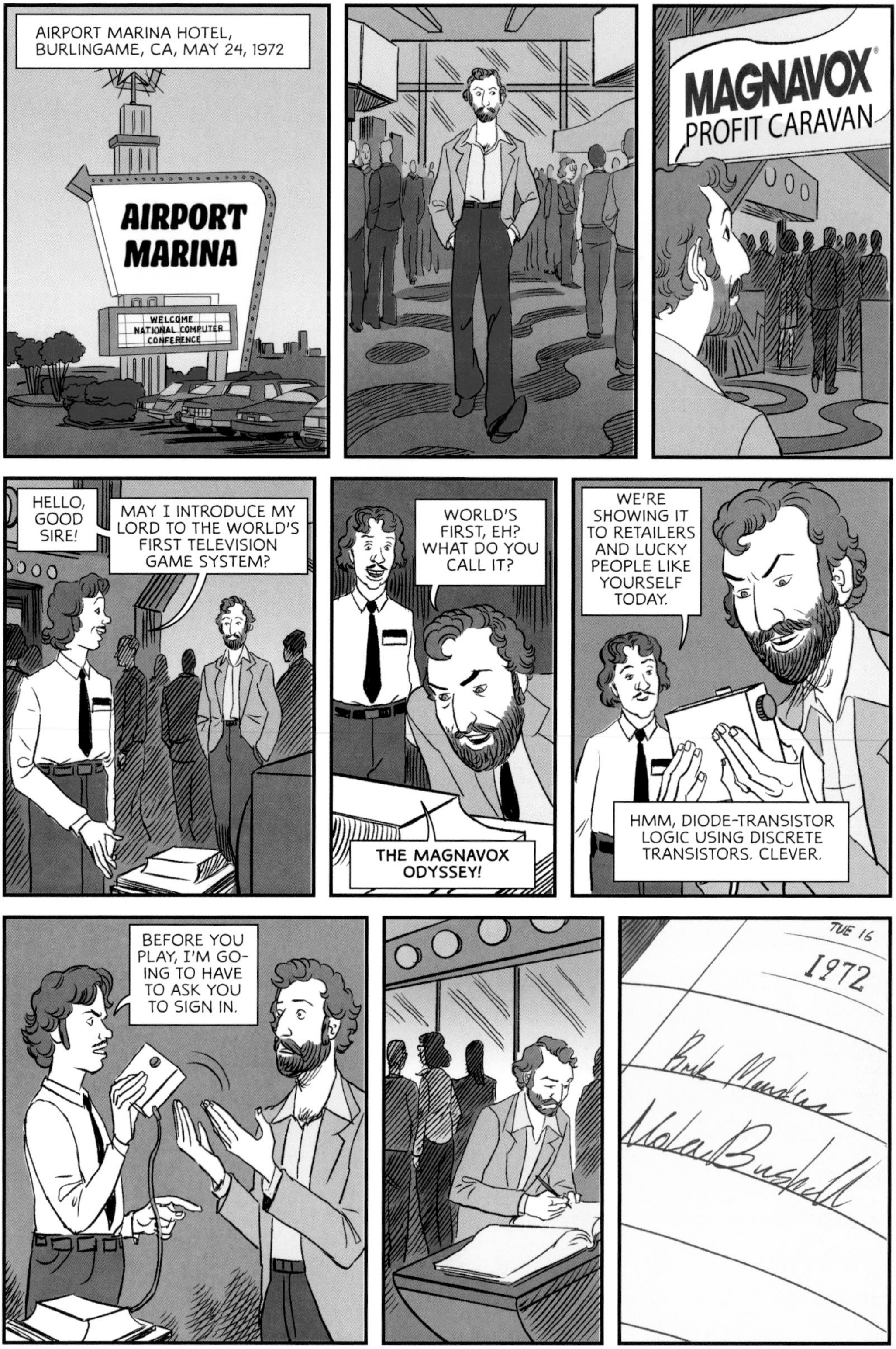
AIRPORT MARINA HOTEL, BURLINGAME, CA, MAY 24, 1972
AIRPORT MARINA
WELCOME NATIONAL COMPUTER CONFERENCE
MAGNAVOX
PROFIT CARAVAN
HELLO, GOOD SIRE!
MAY I INTRODUCE MY LORD TO THE WORLD'S FIRST TELEVISION GAME SYSTEM?
WORLD'S FIRST, EH? WHAT DO YOU CALL IT?
THE MAGNAVOX ODYSSEY!
WE'RE SHOWING IT TO RETAILERS AND LUCKY PEOPLE LIKE YOURSELF TODAY.
HMM, DIODE-TRANSISTOR LOGIC USING DISCRETE TRANSISTORS. CLEVER.
BEFORE YOU PLAY, I'M GOING TO HAVE TO ASK YOU TO SIGN IN.
TUE 16
1972
Nolan Bushnell

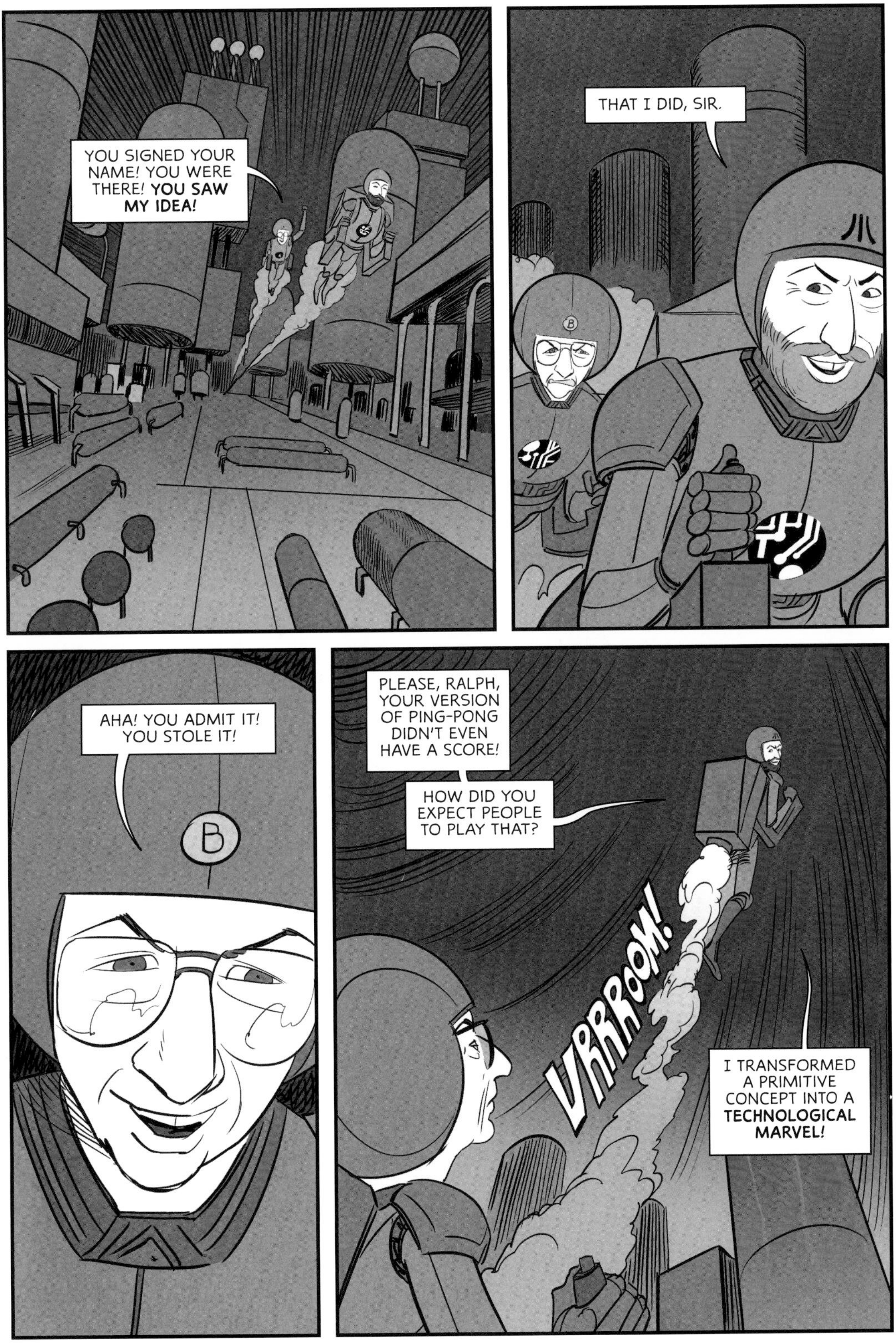
YOU SIGNED YOUR NAME! YOU WERE THERE! **YOU SAW MY IDEA!**
THAT I DID, SIR.
AHA! YOU ADMIT IT! YOU STOLE IT!
PLEASE, RALPH, YOUR VERSION OF PING-PONG DIDN'T EVEN HAVE A SCORE!
HOW DID YOU EXPECT PEOPLE TO PLAY THAT?
VRRROOM!
I TRANSFORMED A PRIMITIVE CONCEPT INTO A **TECHNOLOGICAL MARVEL!**

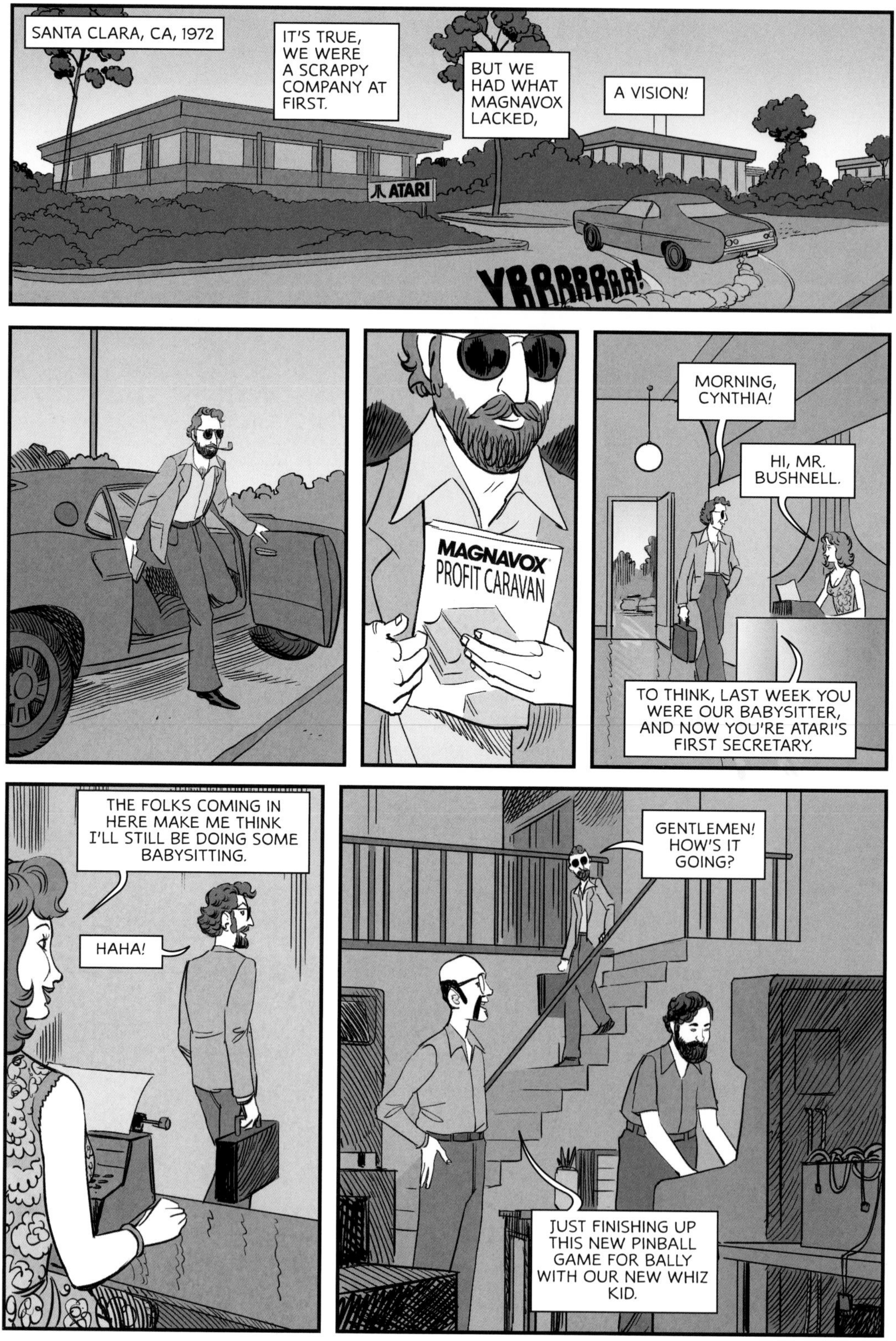
SANTA CLARA, CA, 1972
IT'S TRUE, WE WERE A SCRAPPY COMPANY AT FIRST.
BUT WE HAD WHAT MAGNAVOX LACKED,
A VISION!
ATARI
YRRRRRRR!
MAGNAVOX PROFIT CARAVAN
MORNING, CYNTHIA!
HI, MR. BUSHNELL.
TO THINK, LAST WEEK YOU WERE OUR BABYSITTER, AND NOW YOU'RE ATARI'S FIRST SECRETARY.
THE FOLKS COMING IN HERE MAKE ME THINK I'LL STILL BE DOING SOME BABYSITTING.
HAHA!
GENTLEMEN! HOW'S IT GOING?
JUST FINISHING UP THIS NEW PINBALL GAME FOR BALLY WITH OUR NEW WHIZ KID.

AL ACORN, MEET NOLAN BUSHNELL.

GREAT TO MEET YOU!

WHIZ KID, HUH? I HAVE A NEW JOB FOR YOU, AL!

I JUST GOT A VERY IMPORTANT CALL FROM A VERY IMPORTANT NEW CLIENT: **GENERAL ELECTRIC.**

ALRIGHT!

GE? I THOUGHT THEY--

YESSIR, TED, THAT'S RIGHT! THEY WANT US TO MAKE THEM THAT TABLE TENNIS GAME I'VE LONG BEEN TALKING ABOUT--

AN ELECTRONIC GAME FOR HOMES!

GROOVY! WHAT'S THE GAME?

PING-PONG!

GENERAL ELECTRIC! BY GOLLY! THIS IS BIG TIME.

SURE IS!

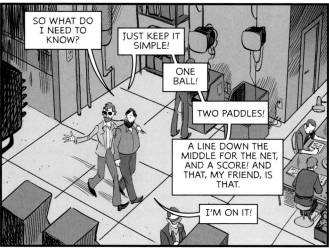

SO WHAT DO I NEED TO KNOW?

JUST KEEP IT SIMPLE!

ONE BALL!

TWO PADDLES!

A LINE DOWN THE MIDDLE FOR THE NET, AND A SCORE! AND THAT, MY FRIEND, IS THAT.

I'M ON IT!

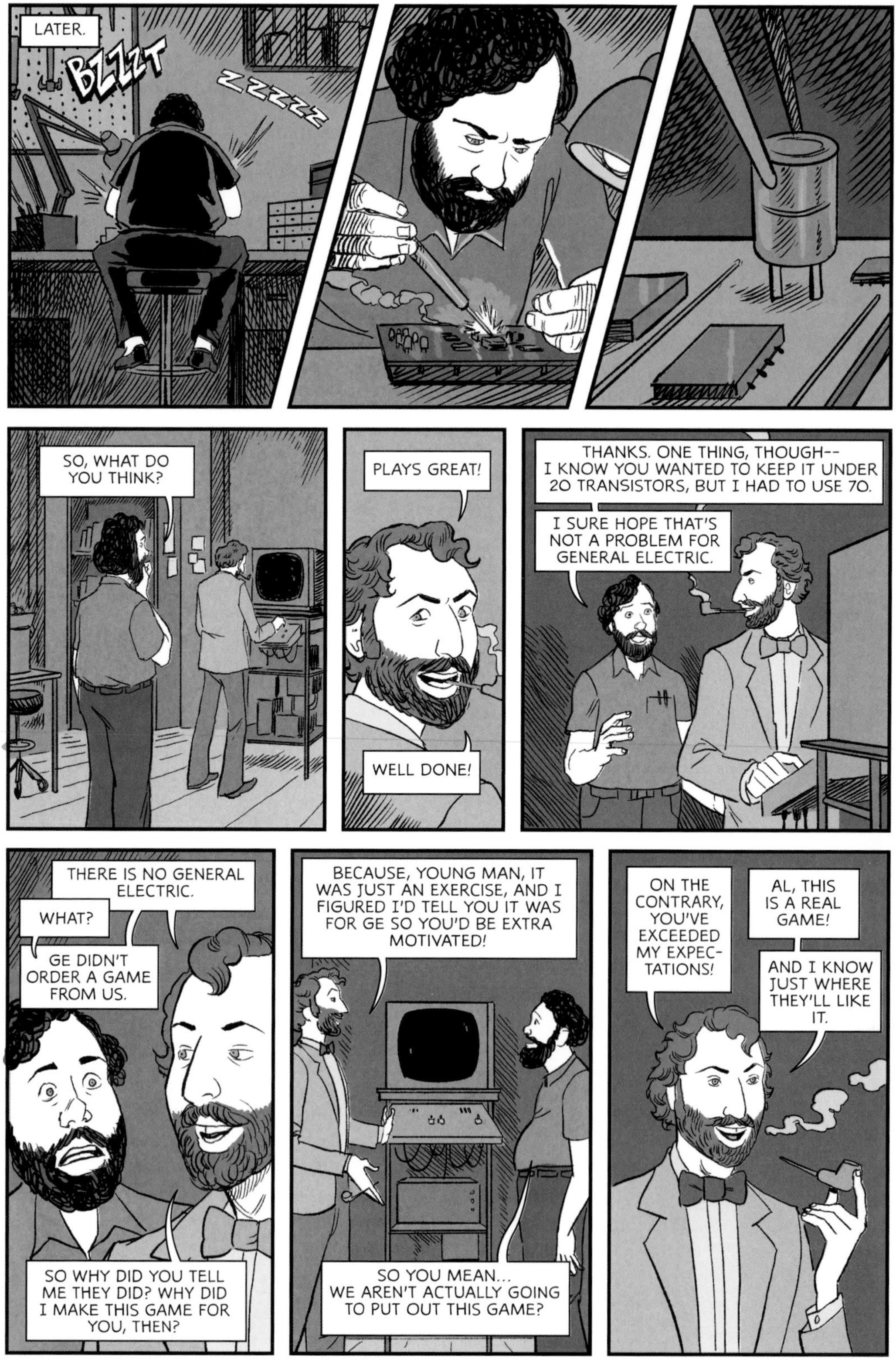
LATER.
BZZZT
ZZZZZZ
SO, WHAT DO YOU THINK?
PLAYS GREAT!
WELL DONE!
THANKS. ONE THING, THOUGH-- I KNOW YOU WANTED TO KEEP IT UNDER 20 TRANSISTORS, BUT I HAD TO USE 70.
I SURE HOPE THAT'S NOT A PROBLEM FOR GENERAL ELECTRIC.
THERE IS NO GENERAL ELECTRIC.
WHAT?
GE DIDN'T ORDER A GAME FROM US.
SO WHY DID YOU TELL ME THEY DID? WHY DID I MAKE THIS GAME FOR YOU, THEN?
BECAUSE, YOUNG MAN, IT WAS JUST AN EXERCISE, AND I FIGURED I'D TELL YOU IT WAS FOR GE SO YOU'D BE EXTRA MOTIVATED!
SO YOU MEAN... WE AREN'T ACTUALLY GOING TO PUT OUT THIS GAME?
ON THE CONTRARY, YOU'VE EXCEEDED MY EXPEC-TATIONS!
AL, THIS IS A REAL GAME!
AND I KNOW JUST WHERE THEY'LL LIKE IT.

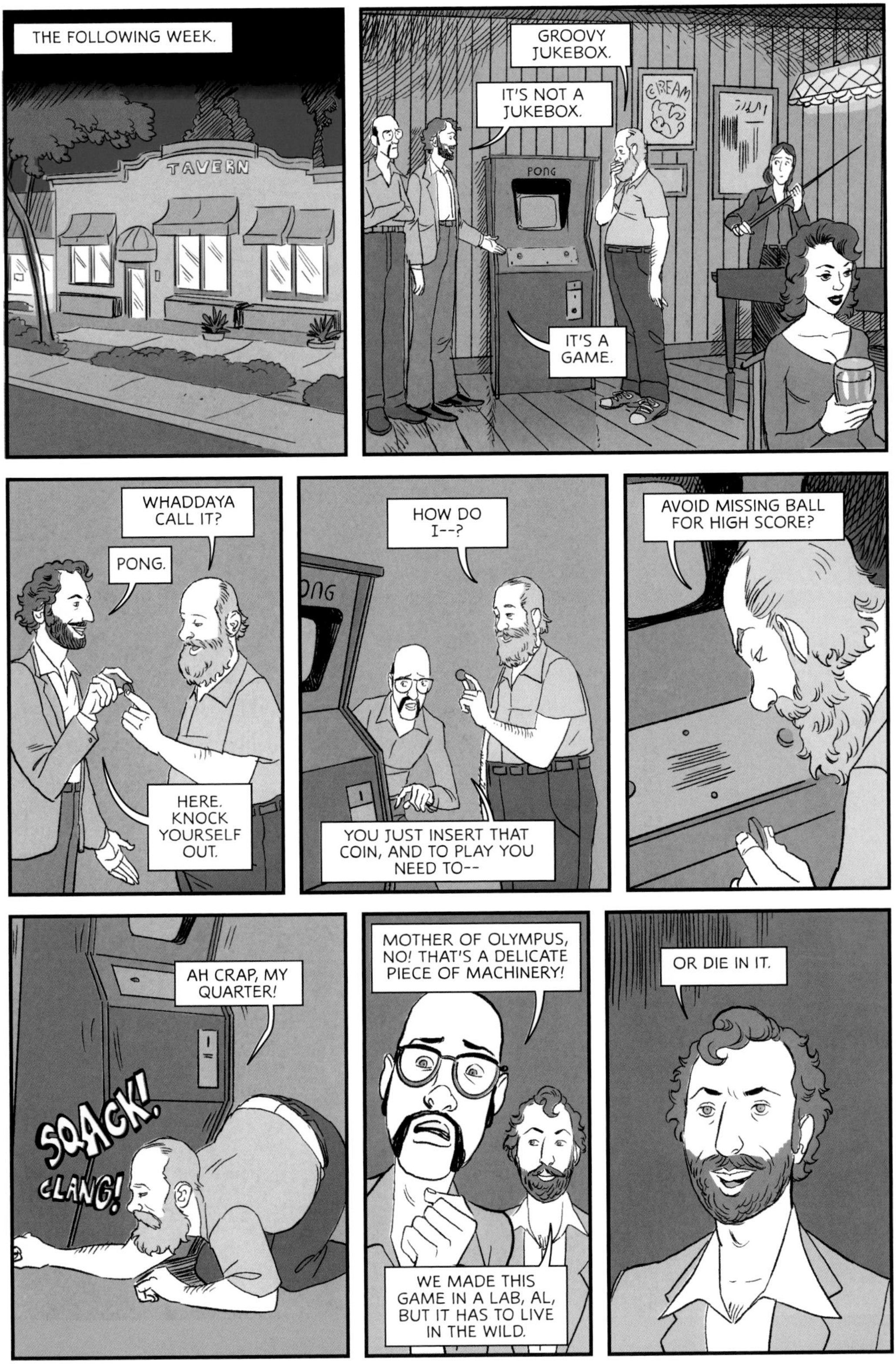
THE FOLLOWING WEEK.
TAVERN
GROOVY JUKEBOX.
IT'S NOT A JUKEBOX.
PONG
IT'S A GAME.
CREAM
WHADDAYA CALL IT?
PONG.
HERE. KNOCK YOURSELF OUT.
HOW DO I--?
YOU JUST INSERT THAT COIN, AND TO PLAY YOU NEED TO--
AVOID MISSING BALL FOR HIGH SCORE?
AH CRAP, MY QUARTER!
SQACK!
CLANG!
MOTHER OF OLYMPUS, NO! THAT'S A DELICATE PIECE OF MACHINERY!
WE MADE THIS GAME IN A LAB, AL, BUT IT HAS TO LIVE IN THE WILD.
OR DIE IN IT.

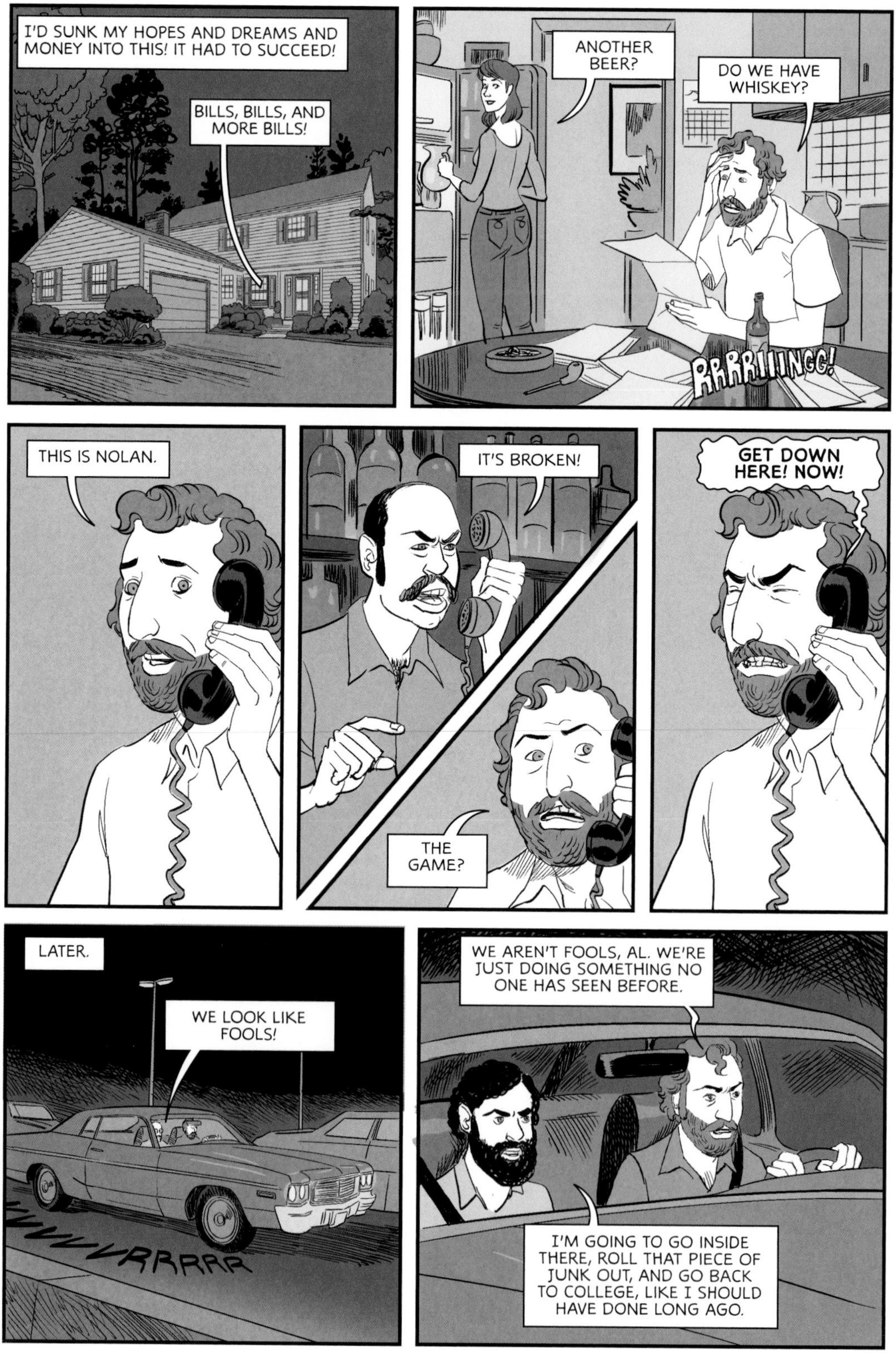
I'D SUNK MY HOPES AND DREAMS AND MONEY INTO THIS! IT HAD TO SUCCEED!
BILLS, BILLS, AND MORE BILLS!
ANOTHER BEER?
DO WE HAVE WHISKEY?
RRRRIIIINGG!
THIS IS NOLAN.
IT'S BROKEN!
THE GAME?
GET DOWN HERE! NOW!
LATER.
WE LOOK LIKE FOOLS!
VVVVVVRRRRRR
WE AREN'T FOOLS, AL. WE'RE JUST DOING SOMETHING NO ONE HAS SEEN BEFORE.
I'M GOING TO GO INSIDE THERE, ROLL THAT PIECE OF JUNK OUT, AND GO BACK TO COLLEGE, LIKE I SHOULD HAVE DONE LONG AGO.

ELECTRONIC ARCADE GAMES! WHAT A JOKE.

WHAT'S WRONG WITH DARTS?

AND GIVE ME MY QUARTERS BACK.

RELAX, ANDY, AL'S CHECKING HER OUT.

IT'S JAMMED.

SEE, BROKEN!

UGHHHH

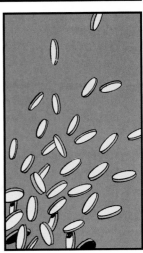

IT WASN'T BROKEN!

IT WAS FULL!

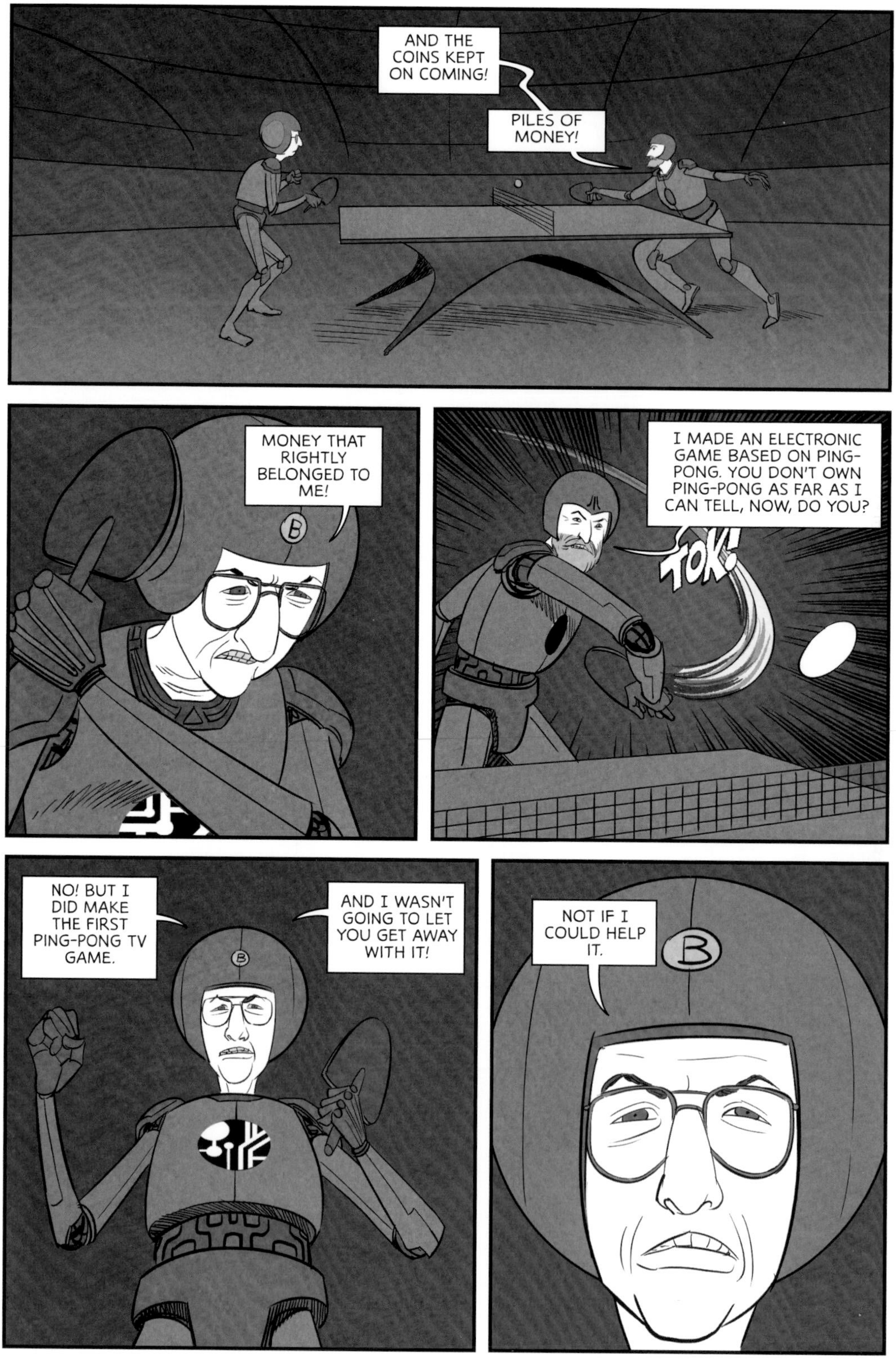
AND THE COINS KEPT ON COMING!
PILES OF MONEY!
MONEY THAT RIGHTLY BELONGED TO ME!
I MADE AN ELECTRONIC GAME BASED ON PING-PONG. YOU DON'T OWN PING-PONG AS FAR AS I CAN TELL, NOW, DO YOU?
TOK!
NO! BUT I DID MAKE THE FIRST PING-PONG TV GAME.
AND I WASN'T GOING TO LET YOU GET AWAY WITH IT!
NOT IF I COULD HELP IT.

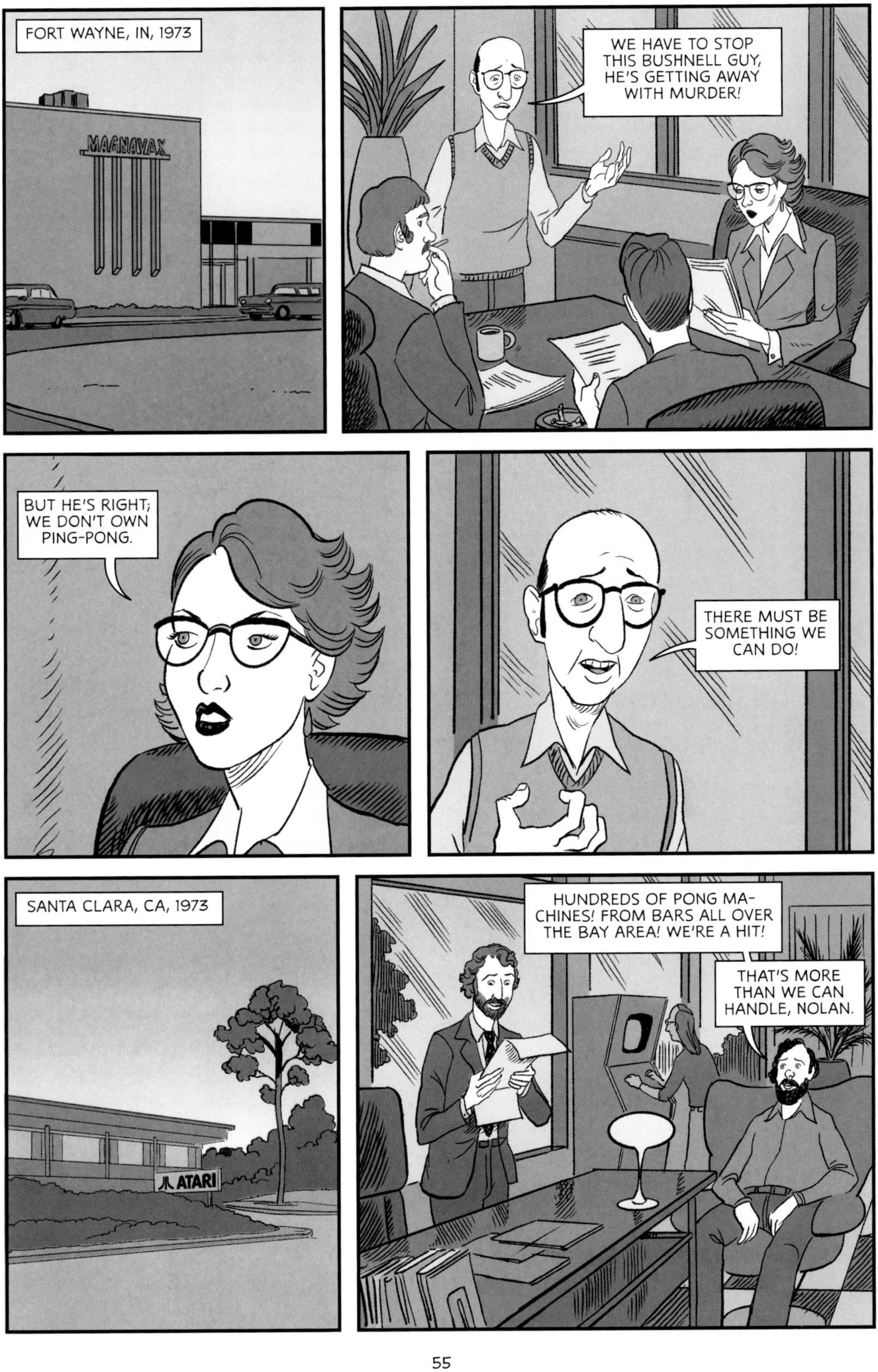
FORT WAYNE, IN, 1973
MAGNAVOX
WE HAVE TO STOP THIS BUSHNELL GUY, HE'S GETTING AWAY WITH MURDER!
BUT HE'S RIGHT; WE DON'T OWN PING-PONG.
THERE MUST BE SOMETHING WE CAN DO!
SANTA CLARA, CA, 1973
ATARI
HUNDREDS OF PONG MA-CHINES! FROM BARS ALL OVER THE BAY AREA! WE'RE A HIT!
THAT'S MORE THAN WE CAN HANDLE, NOLAN.

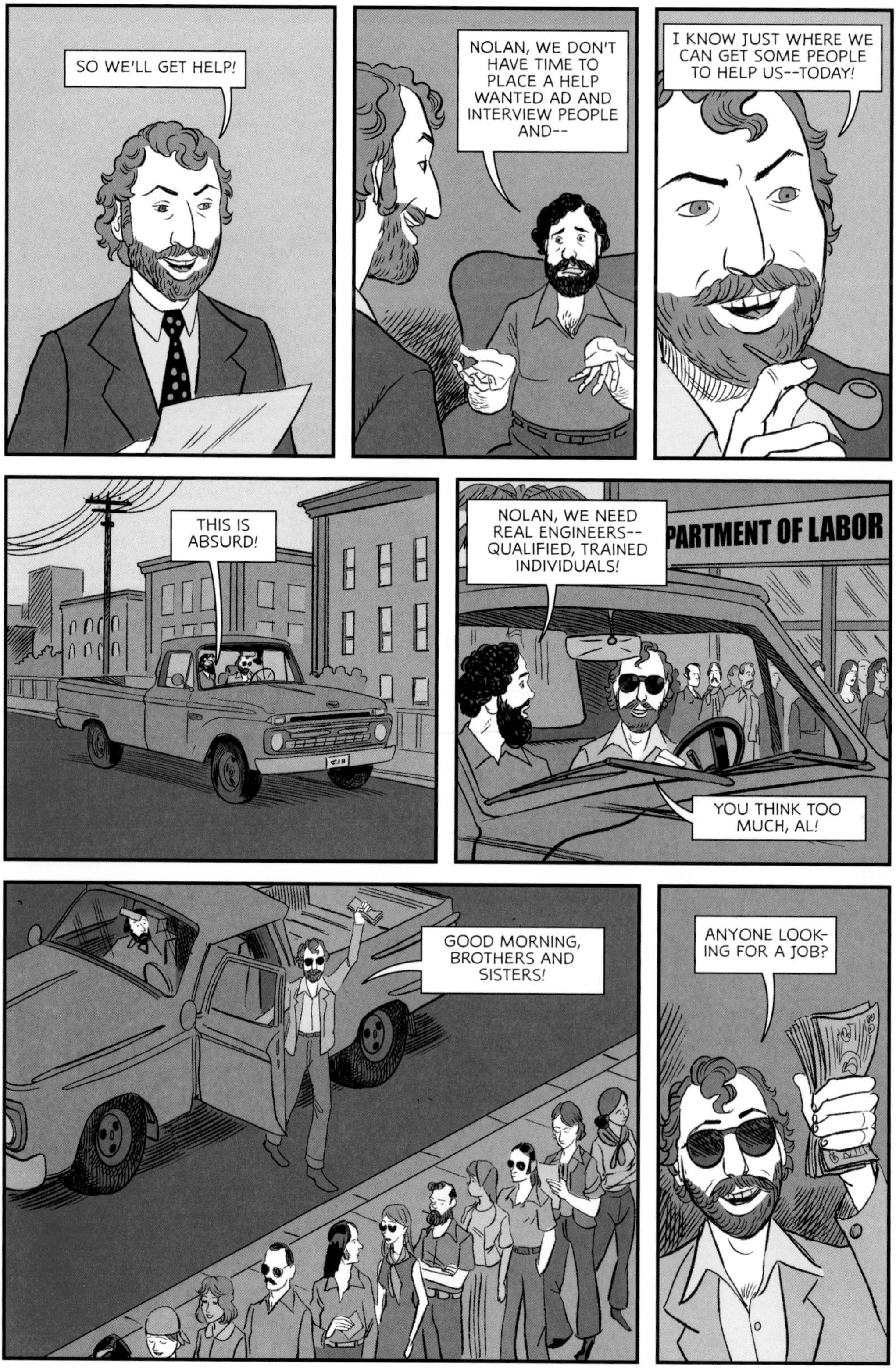
SO WE'LL GET HELP!
NOLAN, WE DON'T HAVE TIME TO PLACE A HELP WANTED AD AND INTERVIEW PEOPLE AND--
I KNOW JUST WHERE WE CAN GET SOME PEOPLE TO HELP US--TODAY!
THIS IS ABSURD!
PARTMENT OF LABOR
NOLAN, WE NEED REAL ENGINEERS--QUALIFIED, TRAINED INDIVIDUALS!
YOU THINK TOO MUCH, AL!
GOOD MORNING, BROTHERS AND SISTERS!
ANYONE LOOK-ING FOR A JOB?

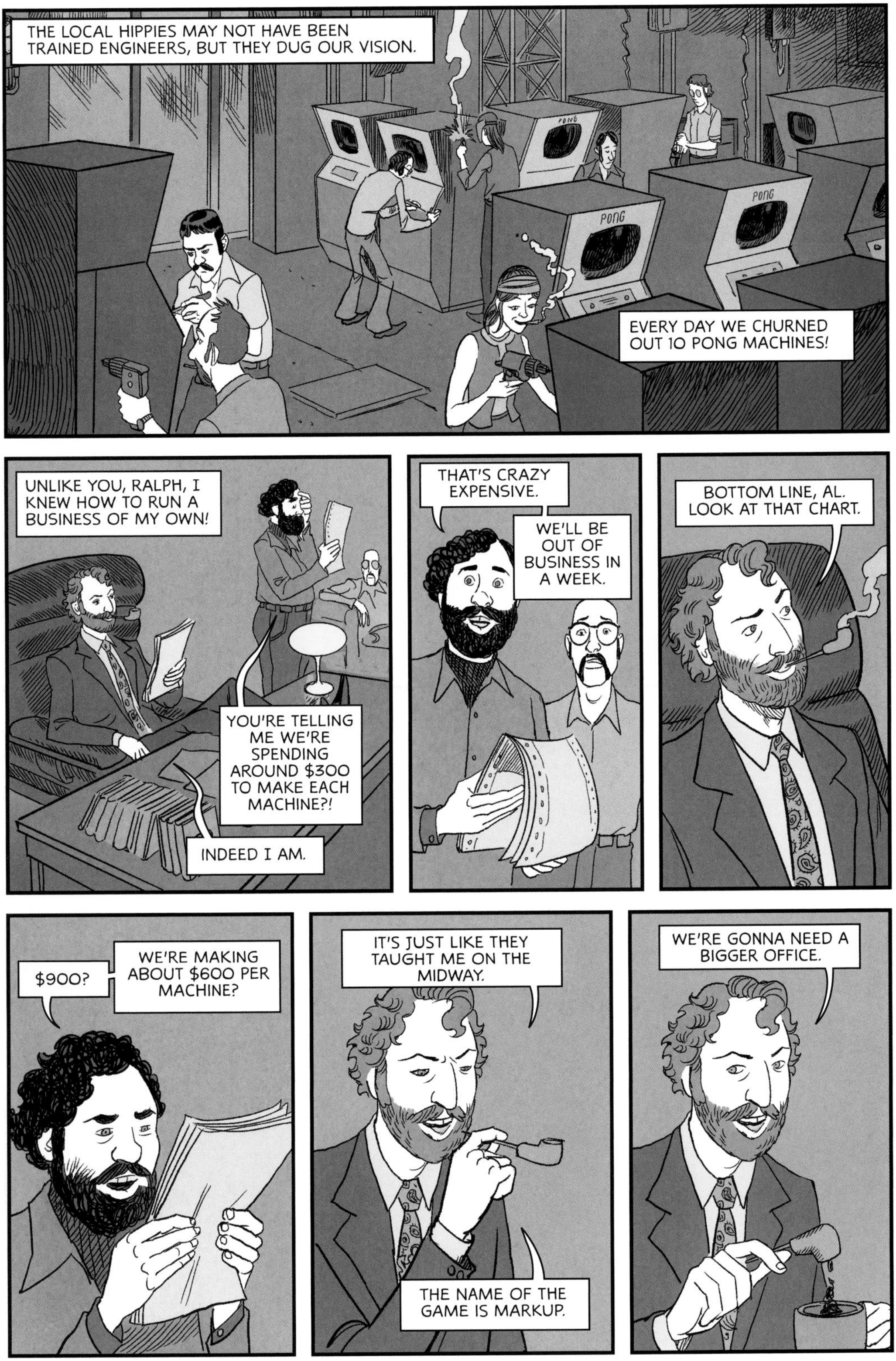
THE LOCAL HIPPIES MAY NOT HAVE BEEN TRAINED ENGINEERS, BUT THEY DUG OUR VISION.
PONG
PONG
PONG
PONG
EVERY DAY WE CHURNED OUT 10 PONG MACHINES!
UNLIKE YOU, RALPH, I KNEW HOW TO RUN A BUSINESS OF MY OWN!
YOU'RE TELLING ME WE'RE SPENDING AROUND $300 TO MAKE EACH MACHINE?!
INDEED I AM.
THAT'S CRAZY EXPENSIVE.
WE'LL BE OUT OF BUSINESS IN A WEEK.
BOTTOM LINE, AL. LOOK AT THAT CHART.
$900?
WE'RE MAKING ABOUT $600 PER MACHINE?
IT'S JUST LIKE THEY TAUGHT ME ON THE MIDWAY.
THE NAME OF THE GAME IS MARKUP.
WE'RE GONNA NEED A BIGGER OFFICE.

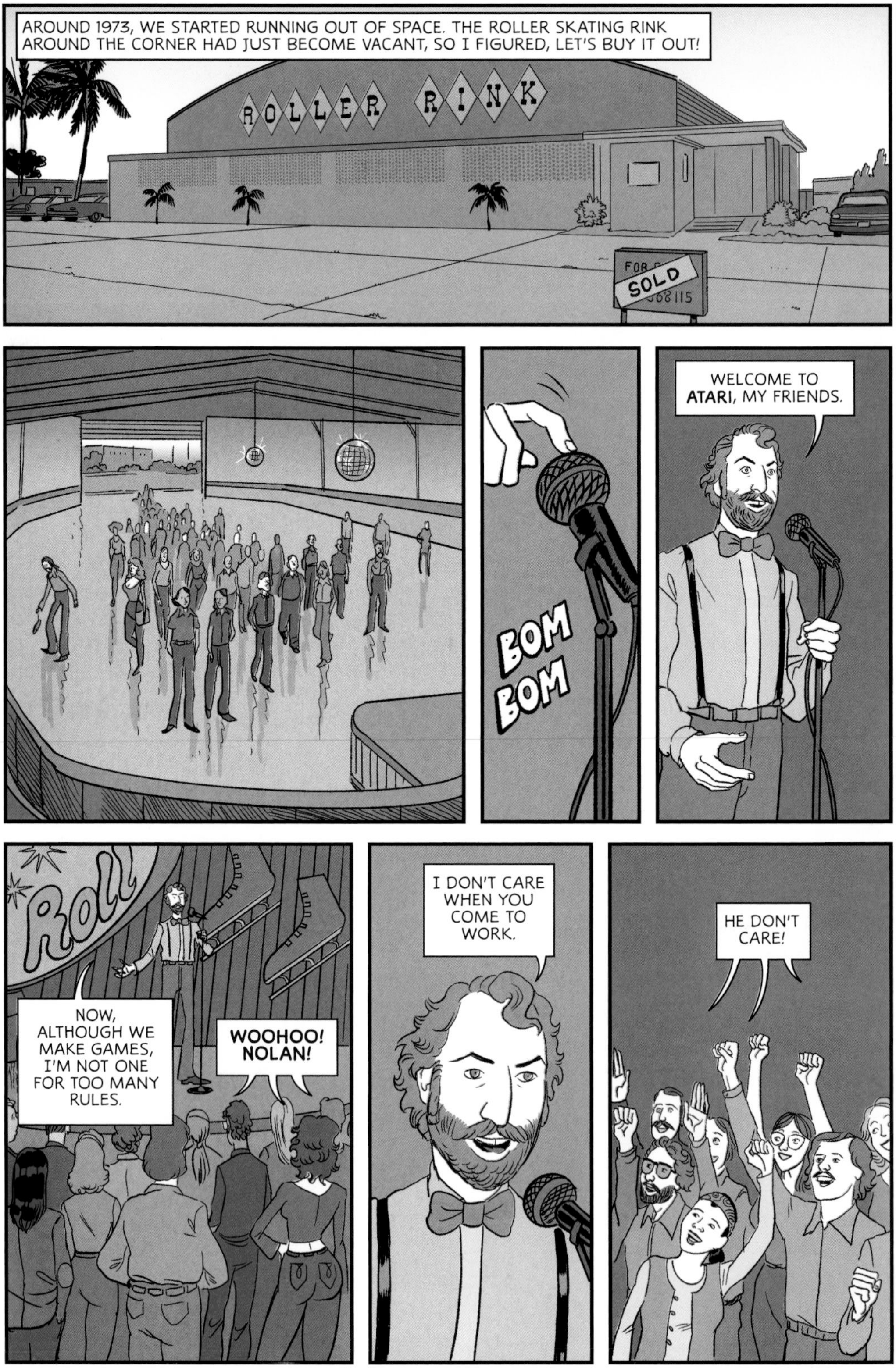
AROUND 1973, WE STARTED RUNNING OUT OF SPACE. THE ROLLER SKATING RINK AROUND THE CORNER HAD JUST BECOME VACANT, SO I FIGURED, LET'S BUY IT OUT!
ROLLER RINK
SOLD
BOM BOM
WELCOME TO ATARI, MY FRIENDS.
NOW, ALTHOUGH WE MAKE GAMES, I'M NOT ONE FOR TOO MANY RULES.
WOOHOO! NOLAN!
I DON'T CARE WHEN YOU COME TO WORK.
HE DON'T CARE!

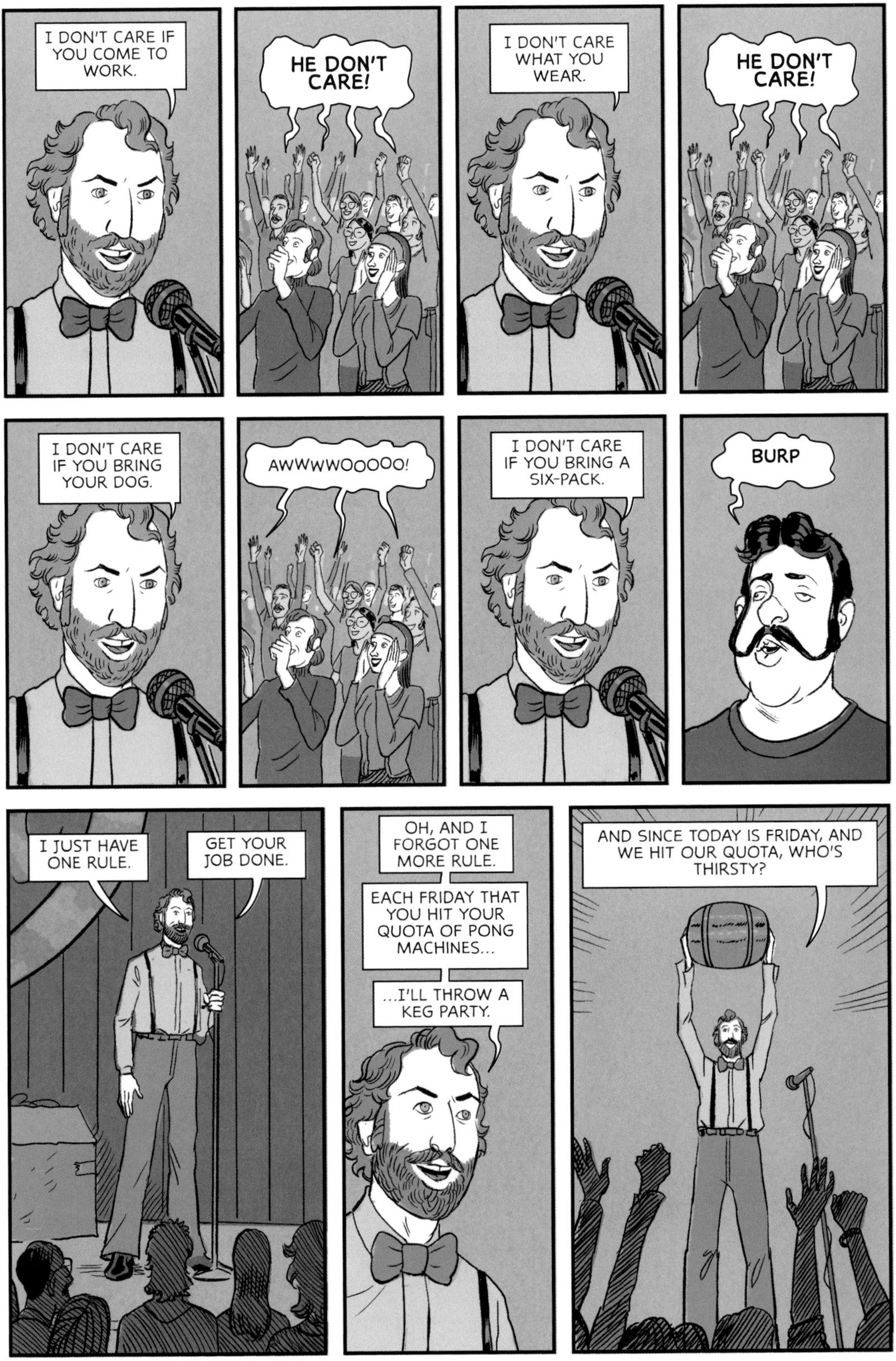
I DON'T CARE IF YOU COME TO WORK.
HE DON'T CARE!
I DON'T CARE WHAT YOU WEAR.
HE DON'T CARE!
I DON'T CARE IF YOU BRING YOUR DOG.
AWWWWOOOOO!
I DON'T CARE IF YOU BRING A SIX-PACK.
BURP
I JUST HAVE ONE RULE.
GET YOUR JOB DONE.
OH, AND I FORGOT ONE MORE RULE.
EACH FRIDAY THAT YOU HIT YOUR QUOTA OF PONG MACHINES...
...I'LL THROW A KEG PARTY.
AND SINCE TODAY IS FRIDAY, AND WE HIT OUR QUOTA, WHO'S THIRSTY?

COME ON, SEVEN, SWEET SEVEN.

YES!

NOLAN, WE HAVE A PROBLEM.

WHAT IS IT?

TODAY'S WALL STREET JOURNAL.

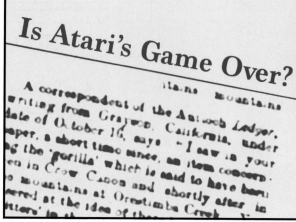

Is Atari's Game Over?

A correspondent of the *Antioch Ledger*, writing from Grayson, California, under date of October 16, says "I saw in your paper, a short time since, an item concerning the 'gorilla' which is said to have been seen in Crow Canon and shortly after in the mountains at Orestimba Creek...

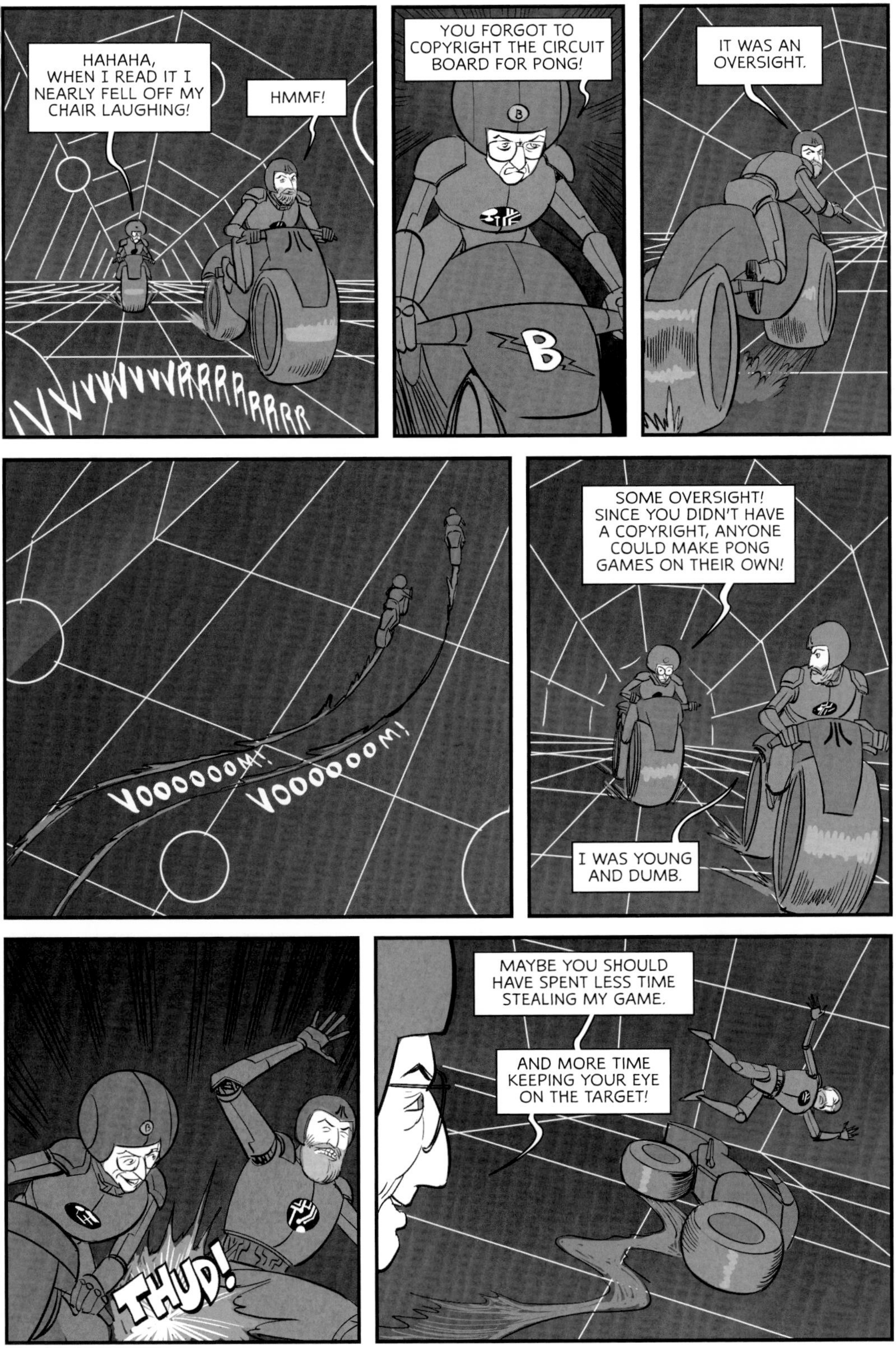
HAHAHA, WHEN I READ IT I NEARLY FELL OFF MY CHAIR LAUGHING!
HMMF!
VVVVVVVVVRRRRRRRRR
YOU FORGOT TO COPYRIGHT THE CIRCUIT BOARD FOR PONG!
B
IT WAS AN OVERSIGHT.
VOOOOOOM!
VOOOOOOM!
SOME OVERSIGHT! SINCE YOU DIDN'T HAVE A COPYRIGHT, ANYONE COULD MAKE PONG GAMES ON THEIR OWN!
I WAS YOUNG AND DUMB.
THUD!
MAYBE YOU SHOULD HAVE SPENT LESS TIME STEALING MY GAME.
AND MORE TIME KEEPING YOUR EYE ON THE TARGET!

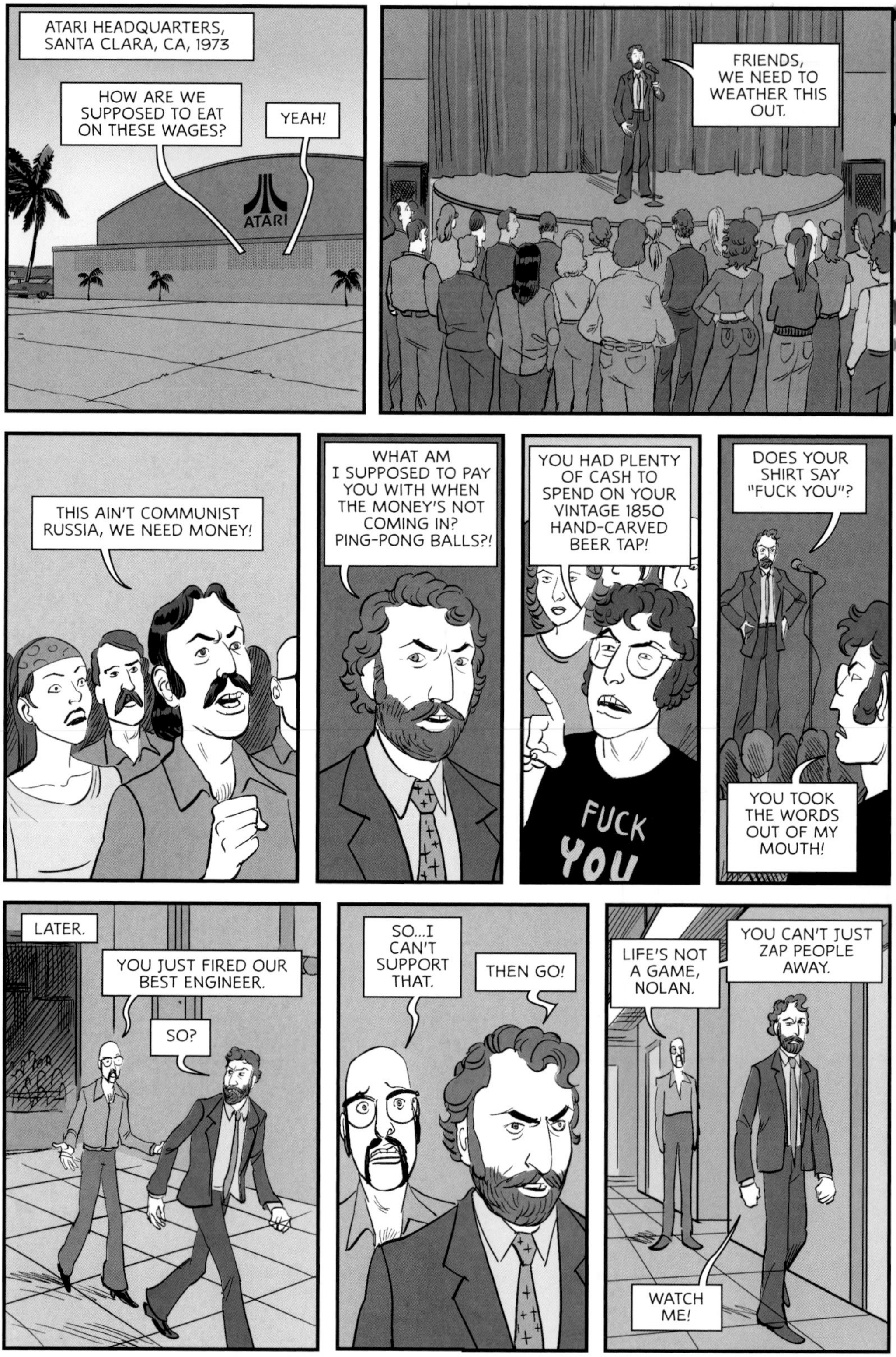
ATARI HEADQUARTERS, SANTA CLARA, CA, 1973
HOW ARE WE SUPPOSED TO EAT ON THESE WAGES?
YEAH!
ATARI
FRIENDS, WE NEED TO WEATHER THIS OUT.
THIS AIN'T COMMUNIST RUSSIA, WE NEED MONEY!
WHAT AM I SUPPOSED TO PAY YOU WITH WHEN THE MONEY'S NOT COMING IN? PING-PONG BALLS?!
YOU HAD PLENTY OF CASH TO SPEND ON YOUR VINTAGE 1850 HAND-CARVED BEER TAP!
FUCK YOU
DOES YOUR SHIRT SAY "FUCK YOU"?
YOU TOOK THE WORDS OUT OF MY MOUTH!
LATER.
YOU JUST FIRED OUR BEST ENGINEER.
SO?
SO...I CAN'T SUPPORT THAT.
THEN GO!
LIFE'S NOT A GAME, NOLAN.
YOU CAN'T JUST ZAP PEOPLE AWAY.
WATCH ME!

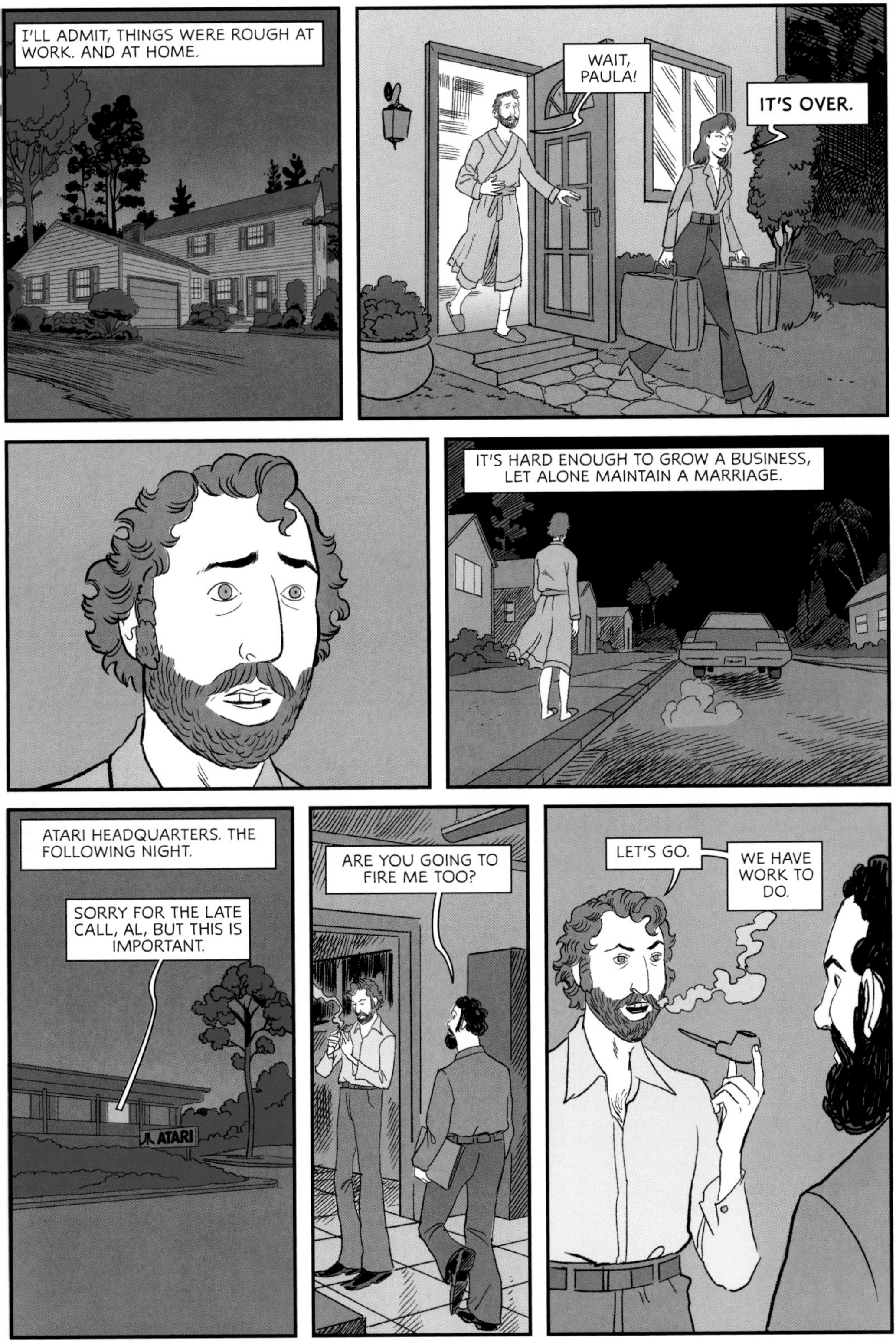
I'LL ADMIT, THINGS WERE ROUGH AT WORK. AND AT HOME.
WAIT, PAULA!
IT'S OVER.
IT'S HARD ENOUGH TO GROW A BUSINESS, LET ALONE MAINTAIN A MARRIAGE.
ATARI HEADQUARTERS. THE FOLLOWING NIGHT.
SORRY FOR THE LATE CALL, AL, BUT THIS IS IMPORTANT.
ATARI
ARE YOU GOING TO FIRE ME TOO?
LET'S GO.
WE HAVE WORK TO DO.

HAND ME THAT C15 CHIP OVER THERE, WILL YOU, AL?

C'MERE LITTLE GUY.

HANG ON, YOU'RE PUTTING THE WRONG NAME ON THAT CHIP!

YOU KNOW, AL, WHEN I WAS A KID, MY NANA MADE THE MOST FANTASTIC APPLE PIE!

EVERYONE WANTED THE RECIPE FOR NANA'S FANTASTIC APPLE PIE! BUT GUESS WHAT? SHE DIDN'T WANT THEM COPYING HER RECIPE,

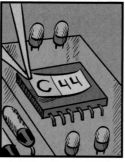

SO GUESS WHAT SHE DID?

SHE GAVE THEM THE WRONG INGREDIENTS.

EXACTLY.

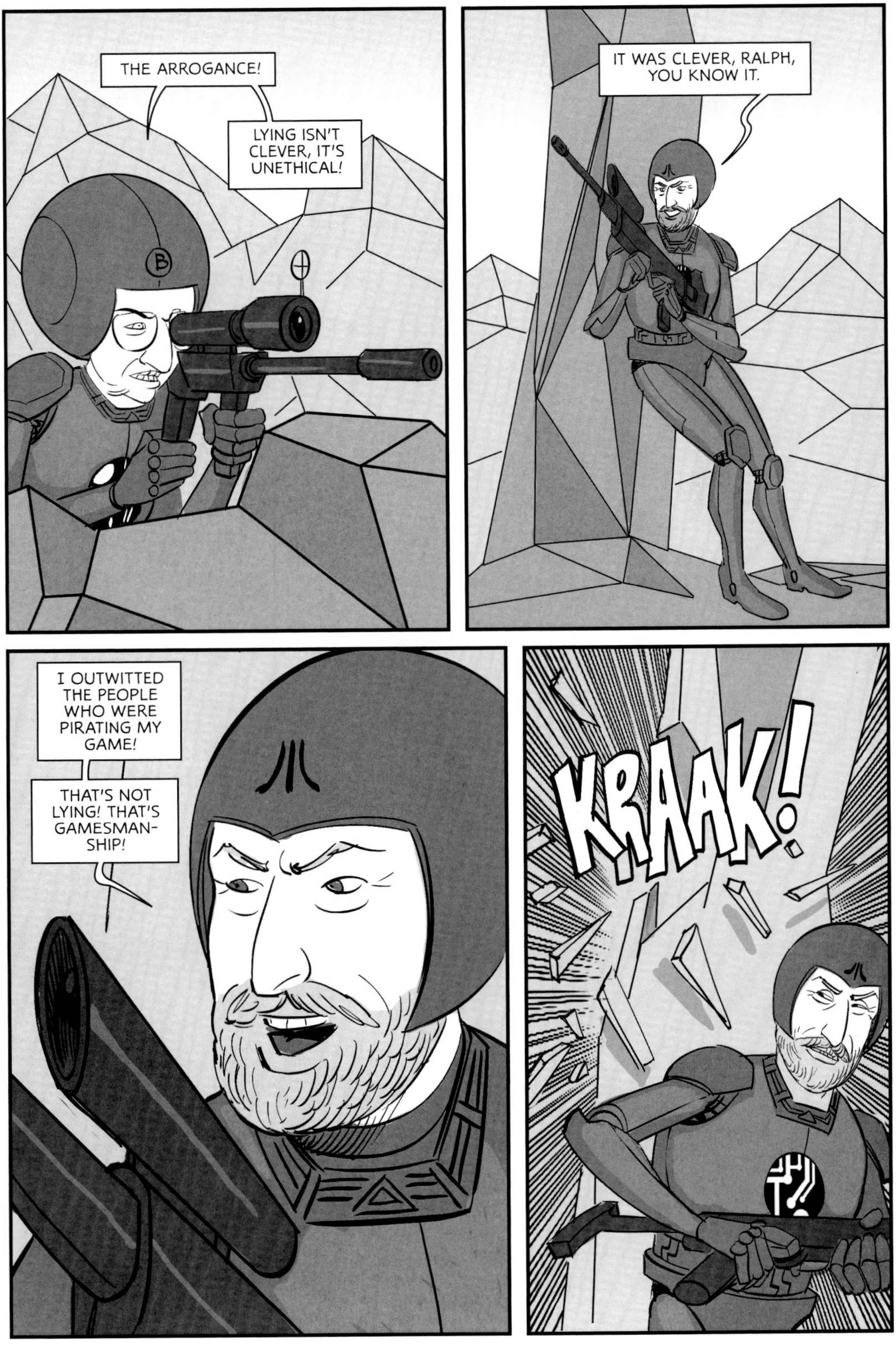
THE ARROGANCE!
LYING ISN'T CLEVER, IT'S UNETHICAL!
IT WAS CLEVER, RALPH, YOU KNOW IT.
I OUTWITTED THE PEOPLE WHO WERE PIRATING MY GAME!
THAT'S NOT LYING! THAT'S GAMESMANSHIP!
KRAAK!

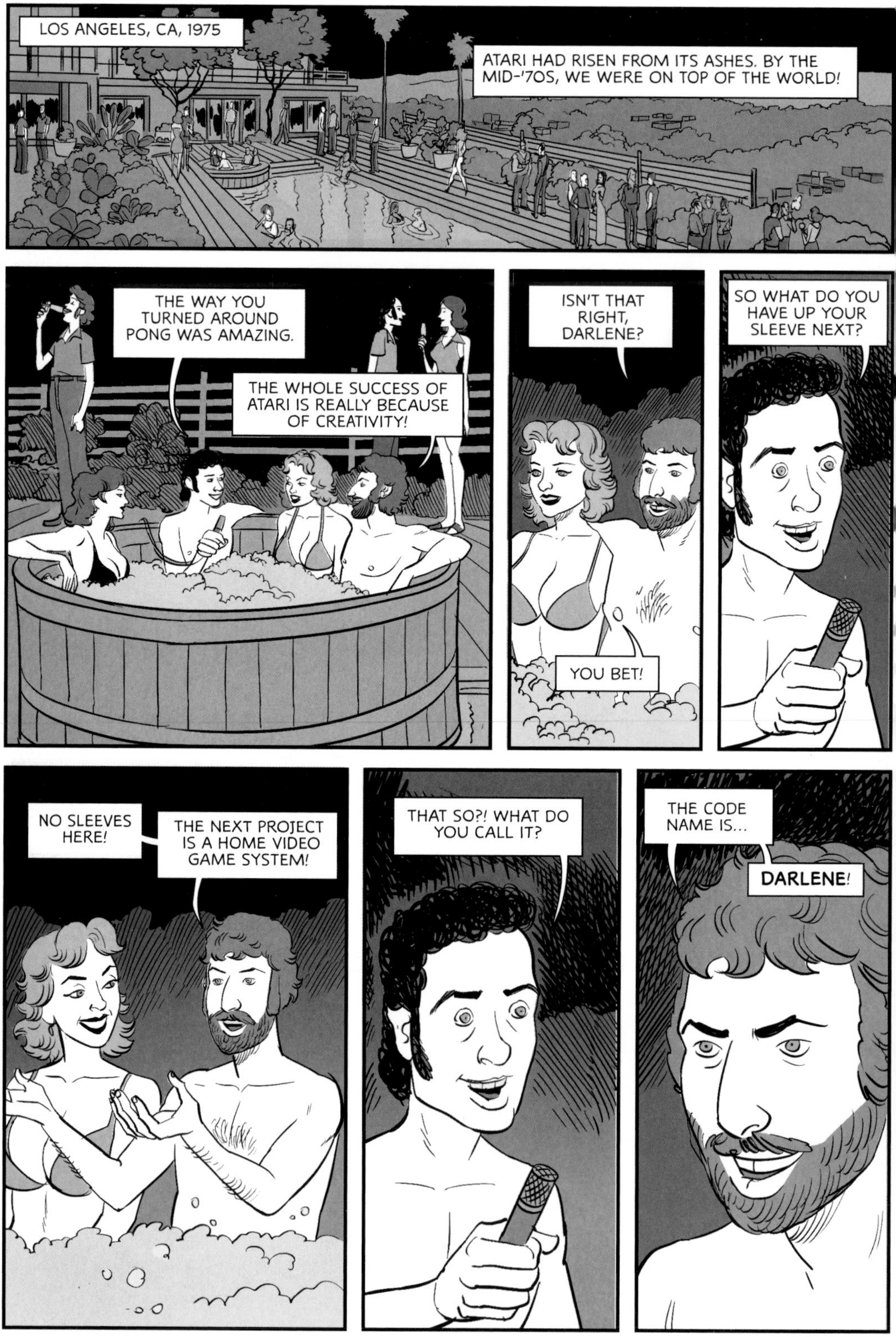
LOS ANGELES, CA, 1975
ATARI HAD RISEN FROM ITS ASHES. BY THE MID-'70S, WE WERE ON TOP OF THE WORLD!
THE WAY YOU TURNED AROUND PONG WAS AMAZING.
THE WHOLE SUCCESS OF ATARI IS REALLY BECAUSE OF CREATIVITY!
ISN'T THAT RIGHT, DARLENE?
YOU BET!
SO WHAT DO YOU HAVE UP YOUR SLEEVE NEXT?
NO SLEEVES HERE!
THE NEXT PROJECT IS A HOME VIDEO GAME SYSTEM!
THAT SO?! WHAT DO YOU CALL IT?
THE CODE NAME IS...
DARLENE!

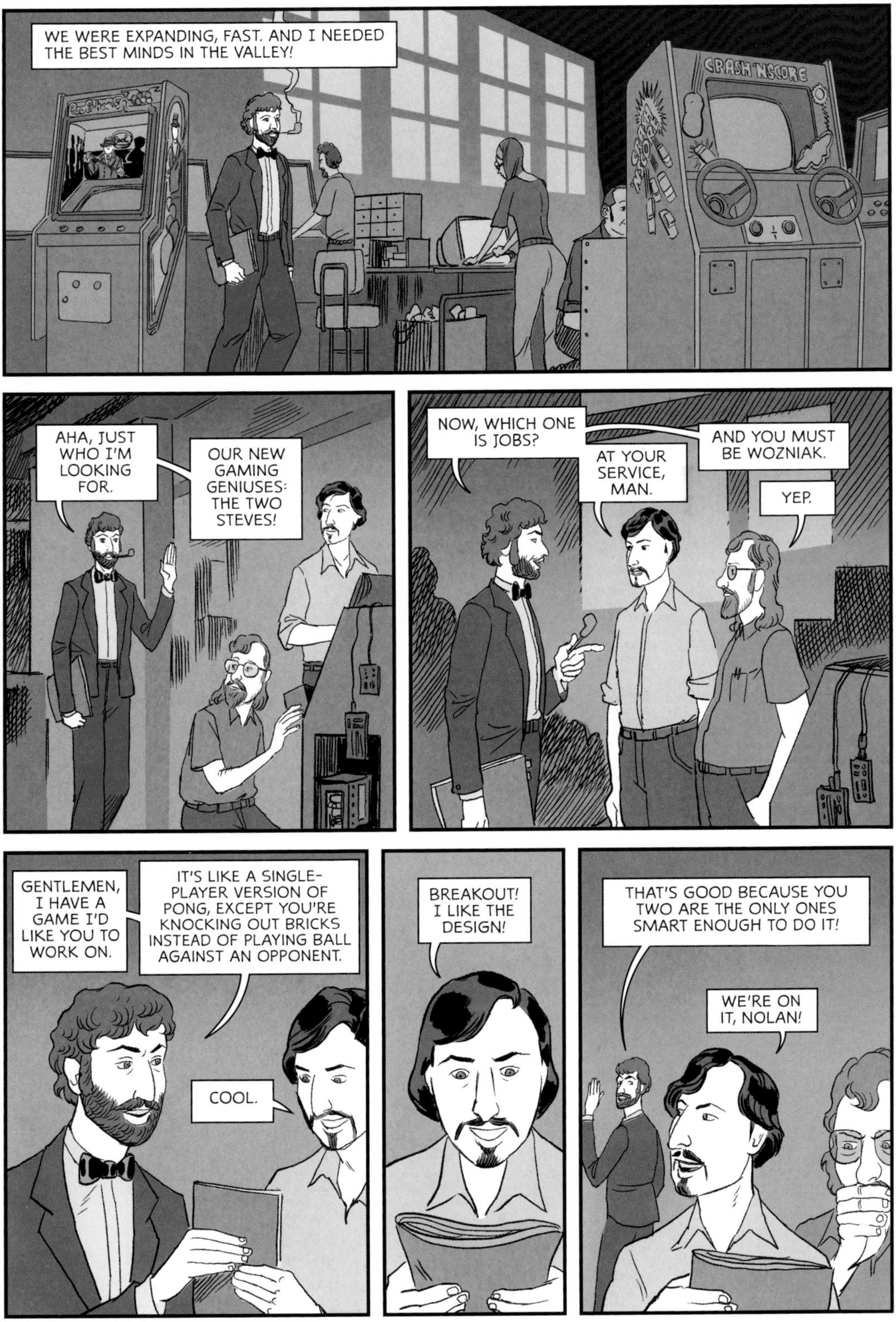
WE WERE EXPANDING, FAST. AND I NEEDED THE BEST MINDS IN THE VALLEY!
CRASH 'N SCORE
AHA, JUST WHO I'M LOOKING FOR.
OUR NEW GAMING GENIUSES: THE TWO STEVES!
NOW, WHICH ONE IS JOBS?
AT YOUR SERVICE, MAN.
AND YOU MUST BE WOZNIAK.
YEP.
GENTLEMEN, I HAVE A GAME I'D LIKE YOU TO WORK ON.
IT'S LIKE A SINGLE-PLAYER VERSION OF PONG, EXCEPT YOU'RE KNOCKING OUT BRICKS INSTEAD OF PLAYING BALL AGAINST AN OPPONENT.
COOL.
BREAKOUT! I LIKE THE DESIGN!
THAT'S GOOD BECAUSE YOU TWO ARE THE ONLY ONES SMART ENOUGH TO DO IT!
WE'RE ON IT, NOLAN!

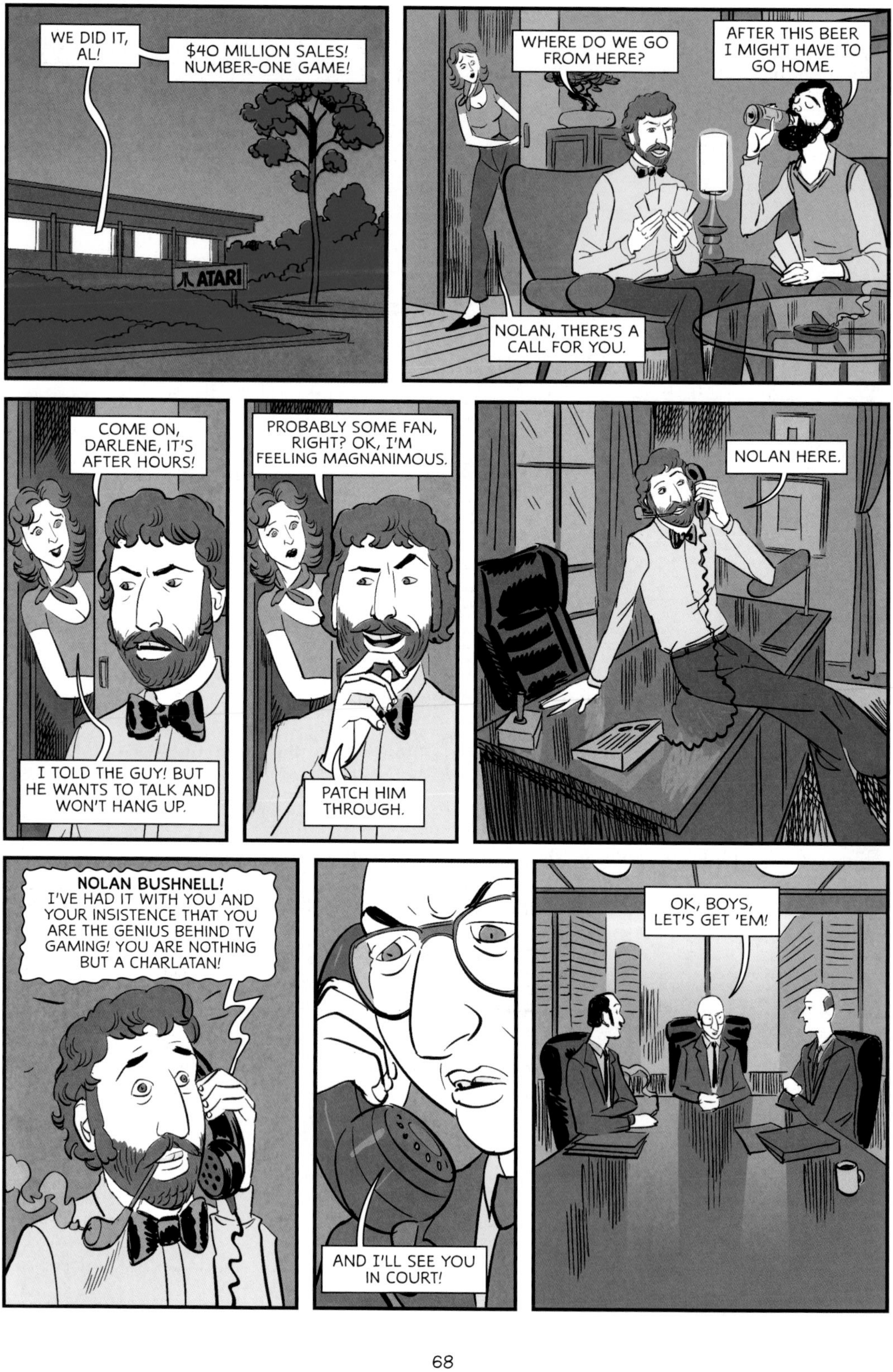
WE DID IT, AL!
$40 MILLION SALES! NUMBER-ONE GAME!
ATARI
WHERE DO WE GO FROM HERE?
AFTER THIS BEER I MIGHT HAVE TO GO HOME.
NOLAN, THERE'S A CALL FOR YOU.
COME ON, DARLENE, IT'S AFTER HOURS!
I TOLD THE GUY! BUT HE WANTS TO TALK AND WON'T HANG UP.
PROBABLY SOME FAN, RIGHT? OK, I'M FEELING MAGNANIMOUS.
PATCH HIM THROUGH.
NOLAN HERE.
NOLAN BUSHNELL! I'VE HAD IT WITH YOU AND YOUR INSISTENCE THAT YOU ARE THE GENIUS BEHIND TV GAMING! YOU ARE NOTHING BUT A CHARLATAN!
AND I'LL SEE YOU IN COURT!
OK, BOYS, LET'S GET 'EM!

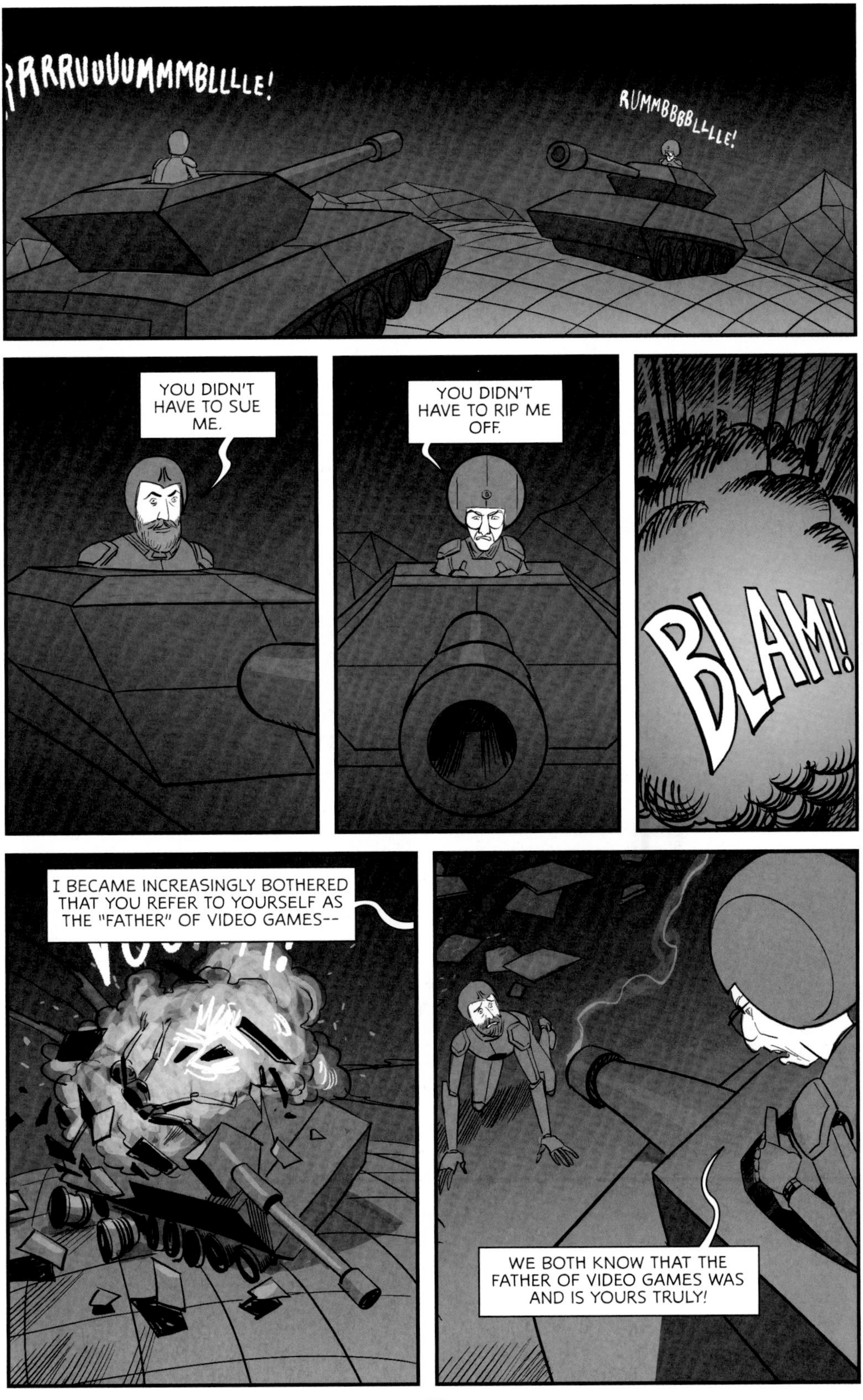
RRRRUUUUMMMBLLLLE!
RUMMBBBBLLLLLE!
YOU DIDN'T HAVE TO SUE ME.
YOU DIDN'T HAVE TO RIP ME OFF.
BLAM!
I BECAME INCREASINGLY BOTHERED THAT YOU REFER TO YOURSELF AS THE "FATHER" OF VIDEO GAMES--
WE BOTH KNOW THAT THE FATHER OF VIDEO GAMES WAS AND IS YOURS TRULY!

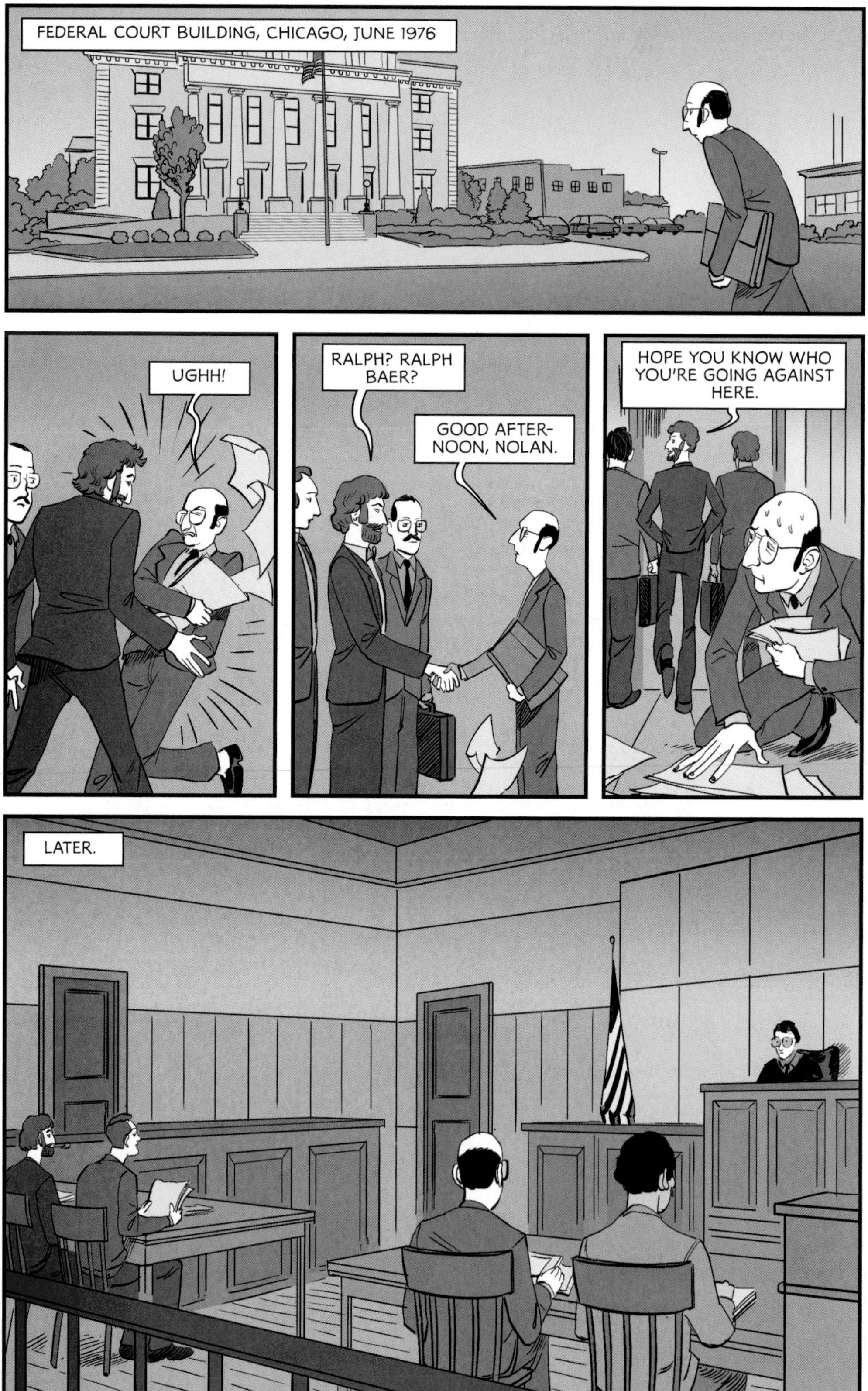
FEDERAL COURT BUILDING, CHICAGO, JUNE 1976
UGHH!
RALPH? RALPH BAER?
GOOD AFTERNOON, NOLAN.
HOPE YOU KNOW WHO YOU'RE GOING AGAINST HERE.
LATER.

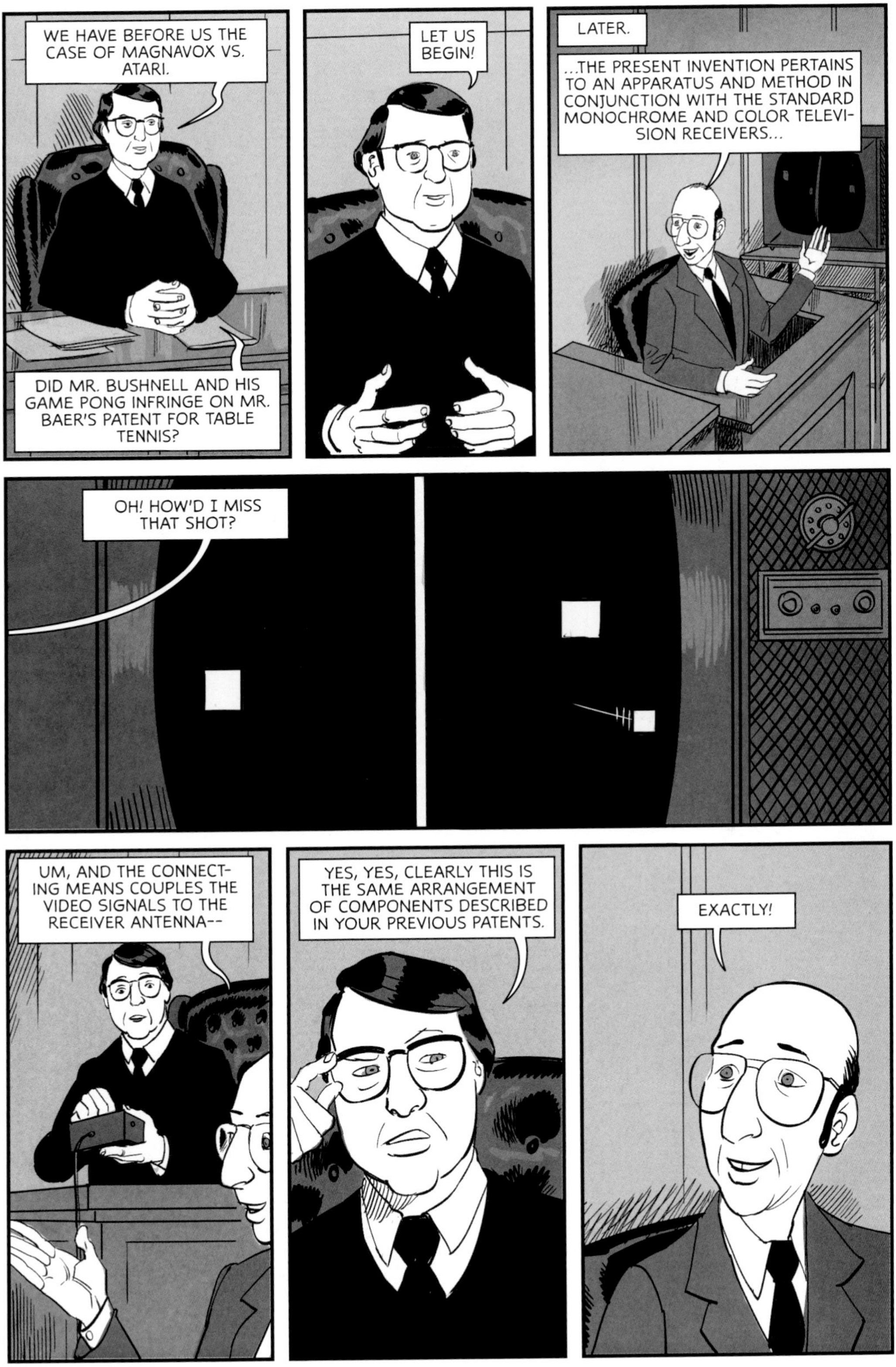
WE HAVE BEFORE US THE CASE OF MAGNAVOX VS. ATARI.
DID MR. BUSHNELL AND HIS GAME PONG INFRINGE ON MR. BAER'S PATENT FOR TABLE TENNIS?
LET US BEGIN!
LATER.
...THE PRESENT INVENTION PERTAINS TO AN APPARATUS AND METHOD IN CONJUNCTION WITH THE STANDARD MONOCHROME AND COLOR TELEVISION RECEIVERS...
OH! HOW'D I MISS THAT SHOT?
UM, AND THE CONNECTING MEANS COUPLES THE VIDEO SIGNALS TO THE RECEIVER ANTENNA--
YES, YES, CLEARLY THIS IS THE SAME ARRANGEMENT OF COMPONENTS DESCRIBED IN YOUR PREVIOUS PATENTS.
EXACTLY!

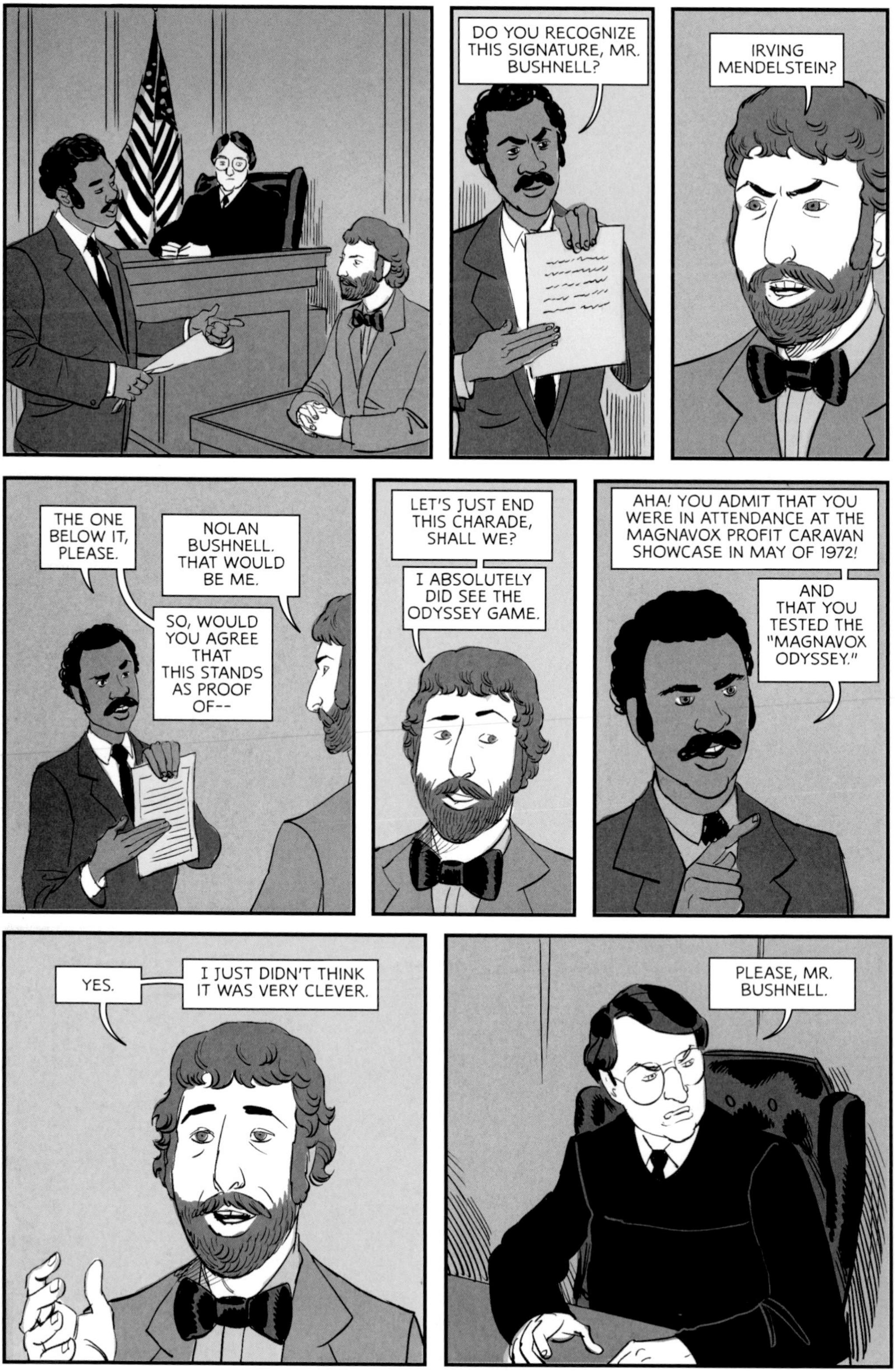
DO YOU RECOGNIZE THIS SIGNATURE, MR. BUSHNELL?
IRVING MENDELSTEIN?
THE ONE BELOW IT, PLEASE.
NOLAN BUSHNELL. THAT WOULD BE ME.
SO, WOULD YOU AGREE THAT THIS STANDS AS PROOF OF--
LET'S JUST END THIS CHARADE, SHALL WE?
I ABSOLUTELY DID SEE THE ODYSSEY GAME.
AHA! YOU ADMIT THAT YOU WERE IN ATTENDANCE AT THE MAGNAVOX PROFIT CARAVAN SHOWCASE IN MAY OF 1972!
AND THAT YOU TESTED THE "MAGNAVOX ODYSSEY."
YES.
I JUST DIDN'T THINK IT WAS VERY CLEVER.
PLEASE, MR. BUSHNELL.

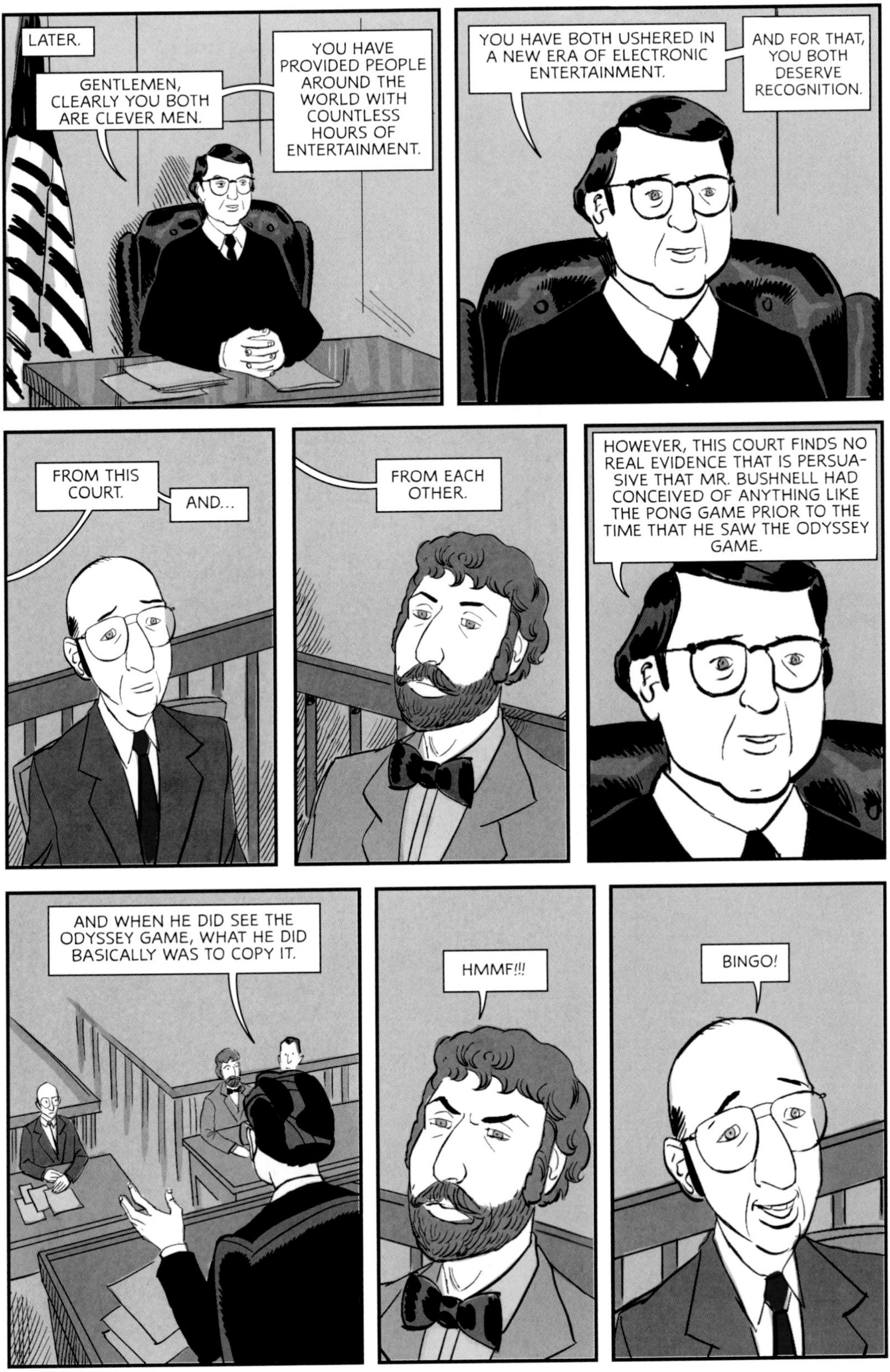
LATER.
GENTLEMEN, CLEARLY YOU BOTH ARE CLEVER MEN.
YOU HAVE PROVIDED PEOPLE AROUND THE WORLD WITH COUNTLESS HOURS OF ENTERTAINMENT.
YOU HAVE BOTH USHERED IN A NEW ERA OF ELECTRONIC ENTERTAINMENT.
AND FOR THAT, YOU BOTH DESERVE RECOGNITION.
FROM THIS COURT.
AND...
FROM EACH OTHER.
HOWEVER, THIS COURT FINDS NO REAL EVIDENCE THAT IS PERSUASIVE THAT MR. BUSHNELL HAD CONCEIVED OF ANYTHING LIKE THE PONG GAME PRIOR TO THE TIME THAT HE SAW THE ODYSSEY GAME.
AND WHEN HE DID SEE THE ODYSSEY GAME, WHAT HE DID BASICALLY WAS TO COPY IT.
HMMF!!!
BINGO!

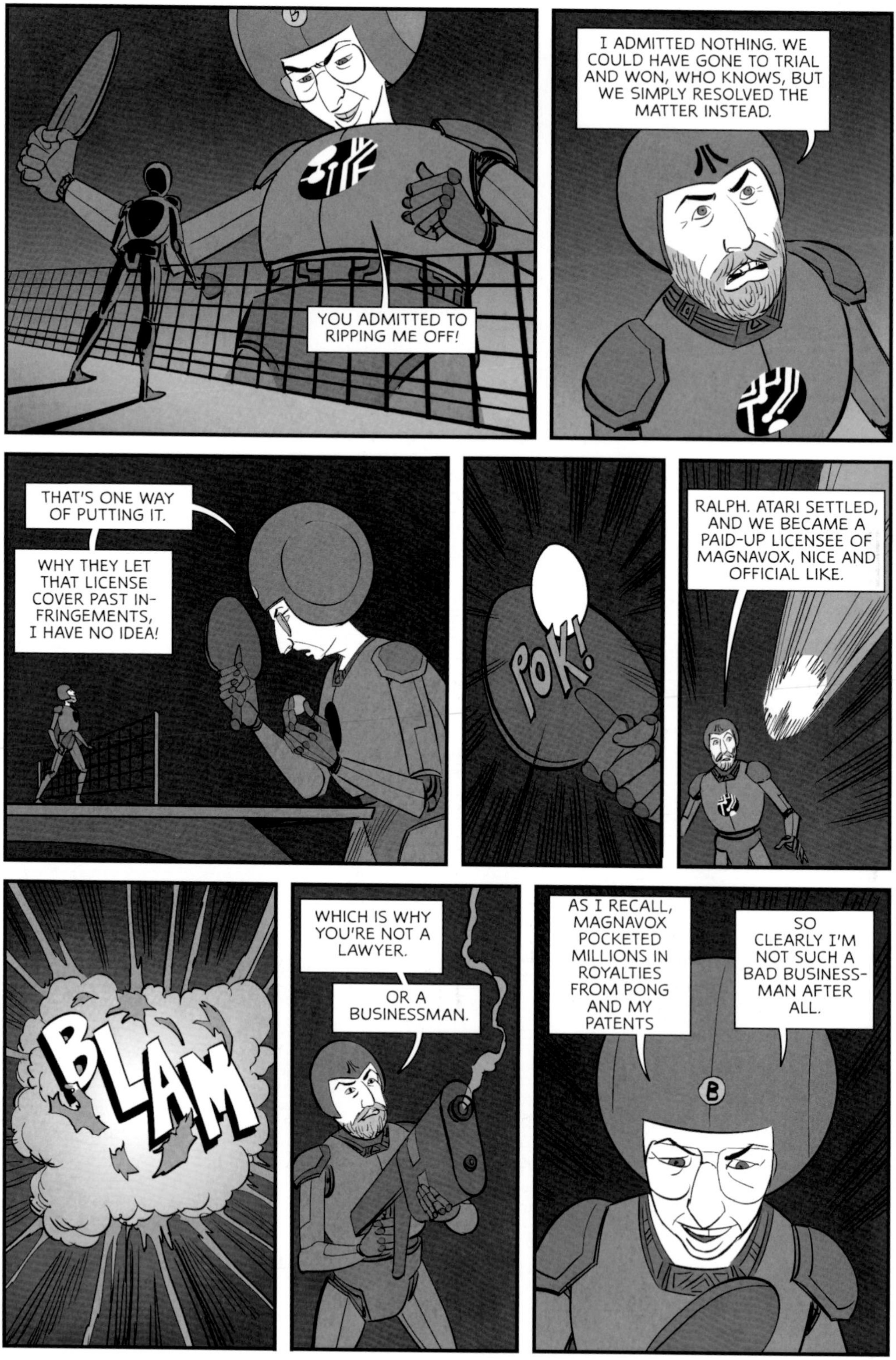
YOU ADMITTED TO RIPPING ME OFF!
I ADMITTED NOTHING. WE COULD HAVE GONE TO TRIAL AND WON, WHO KNOWS, BUT WE SIMPLY RESOLVED THE MATTER INSTEAD.
THAT'S ONE WAY OF PUTTING IT.
WHY THEY LET THAT LICENSE COVER PAST IN-FRINGEMENTS, I HAVE NO IDEA!
POK!
RALPH. ATARI SETTLED, AND WE BECAME A PAID-UP LICENSEE OF MAGNAVOX, NICE AND OFFICIAL LIKE.
BLAM
WHICH IS WHY YOU'RE NOT A LAWYER.
OR A BUSINESSMAN.
AS I RECALL, MAGNAVOX POCKETED MILLIONS IN ROYALTIES FROM PONG AND MY PATENTS
SO CLEARLY I'M NOT SUCH A BAD BUSINESS-MAN AFTER ALL.

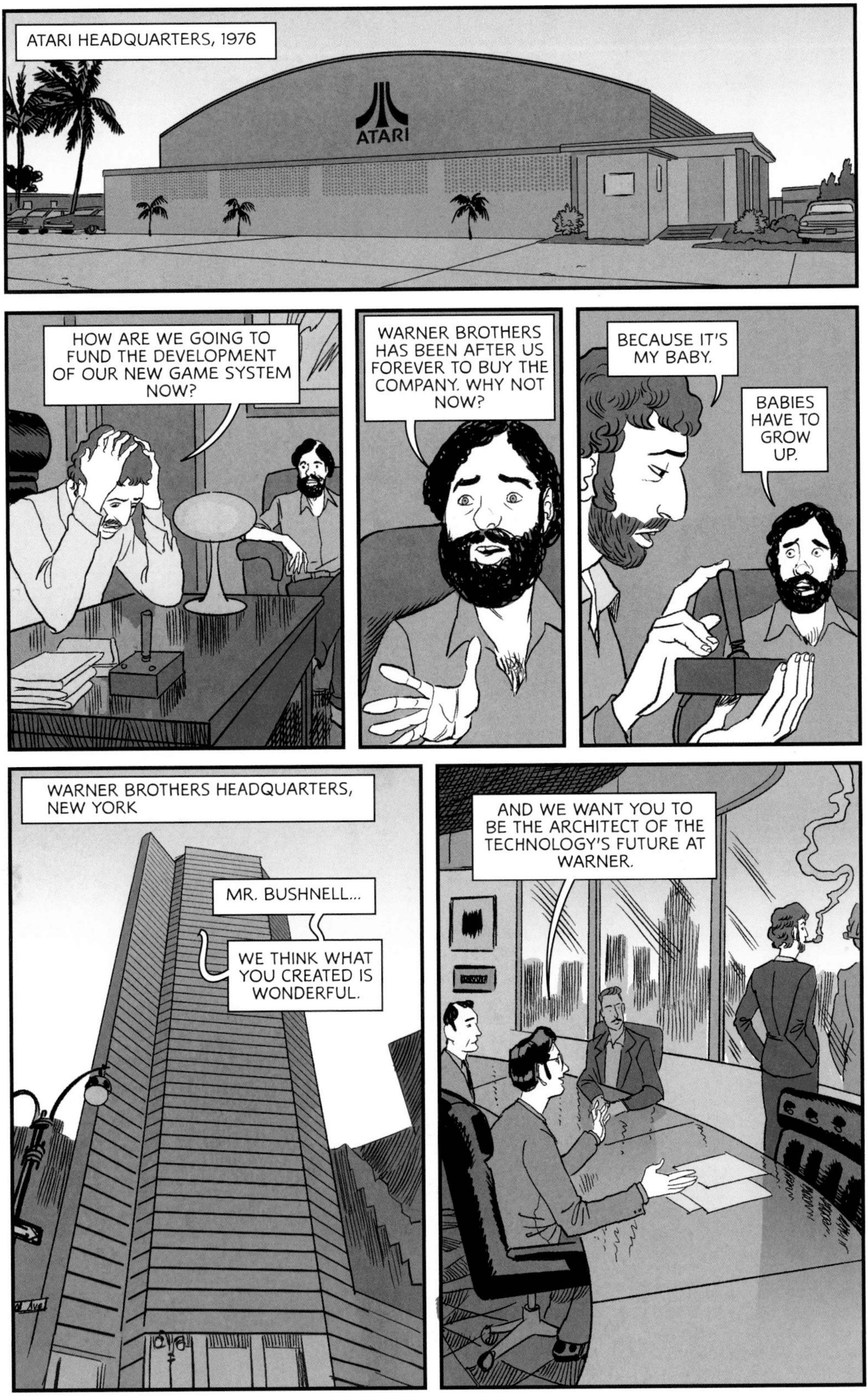

ATARI HEADQUARTERS, 1976
ATARI
HOW ARE WE GOING TO FUND THE DEVELOPMENT OF OUR NEW GAME SYSTEM NOW?
WARNER BROTHERS HAS BEEN AFTER US FOREVER TO BUY THE COMPANY. WHY NOT NOW?
BECAUSE IT'S MY BABY.
BABIES HAVE TO GROW UP.
WARNER BROTHERS HEADQUARTERS, NEW YORK
MR. BUSHNELL...
WE THINK WHAT YOU CREATED IS WONDERFUL.
AND WE WANT YOU TO BE THE ARCHITECT OF THE TECHNOLOGY'S FUTURE AT WARNER.

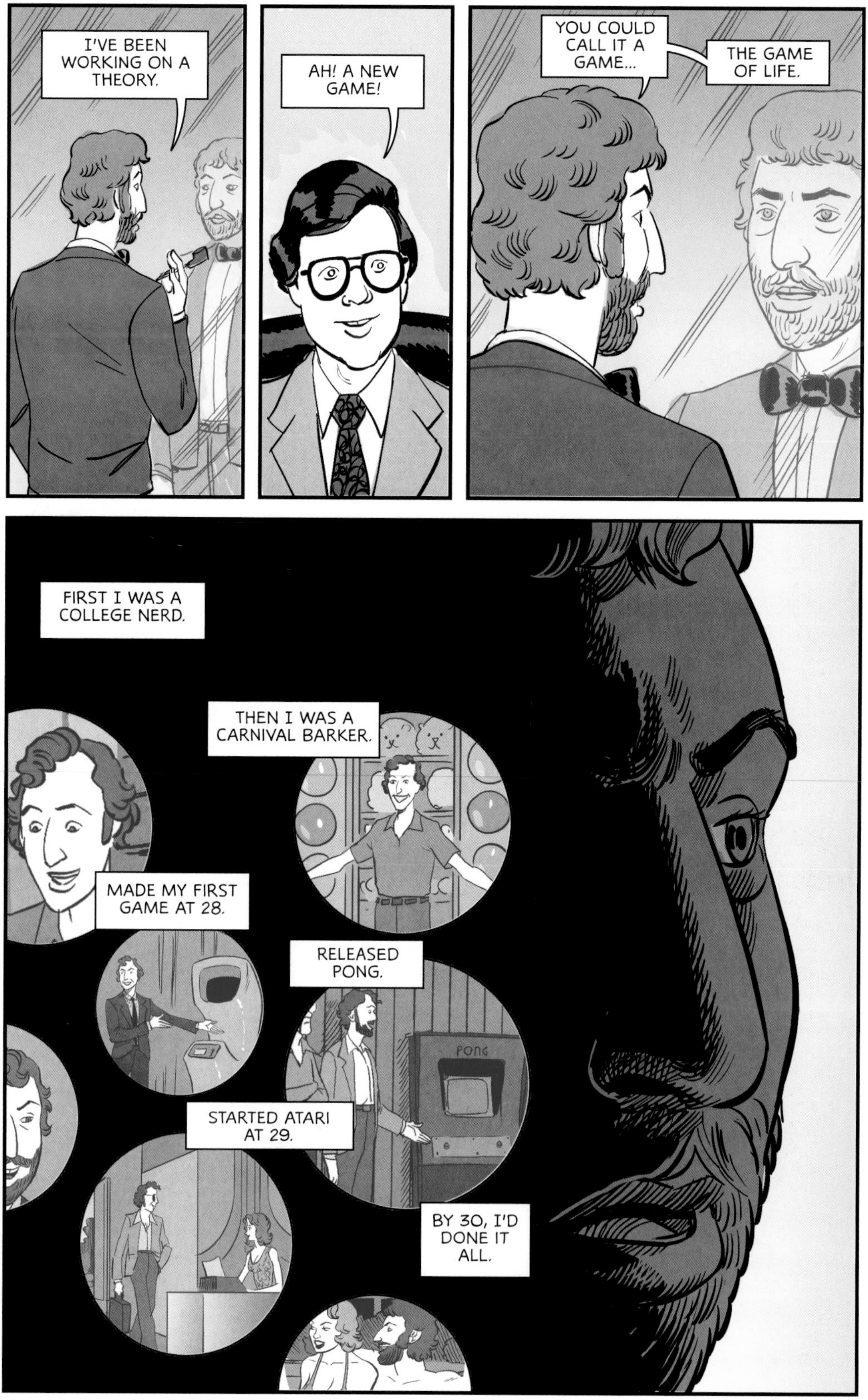
I'VE BEEN WORKING ON A THEORY.
AH! A NEW GAME!
YOU COULD CALL IT A GAME...
THE GAME OF LIFE.
FIRST I WAS A COLLEGE NERD.
THEN I WAS A CARNIVAL BARKER.
MADE MY FIRST GAME AT 28.
RELEASED PONG.
PONG
STARTED ATARI AT 29.
BY 30, I'D DONE IT ALL.

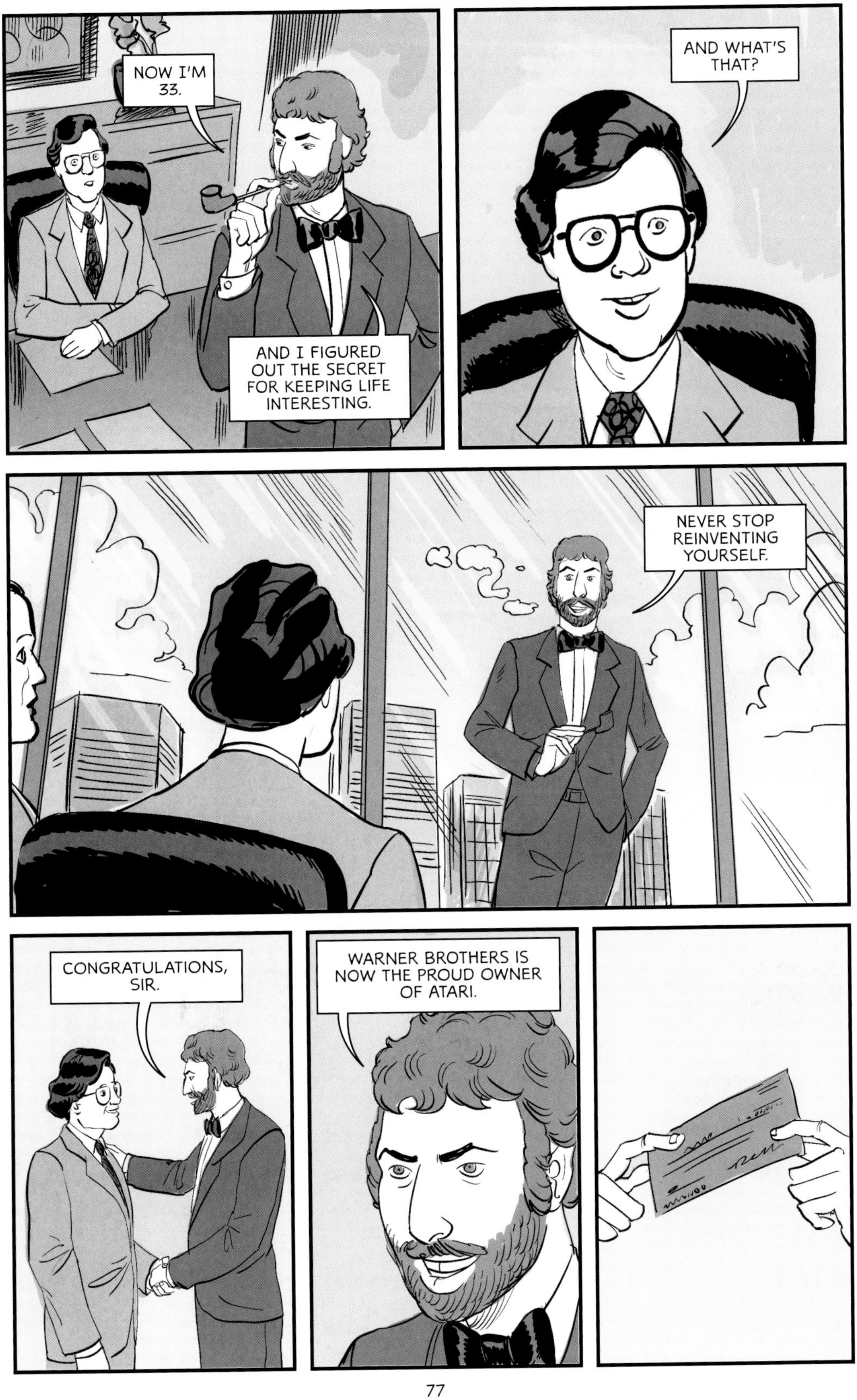
NOW I'M 33.
AND I FIGURED OUT THE SECRET FOR KEEPING LIFE INTERESTING.
AND WHAT'S THAT?
NEVER STOP REINVENTING YOURSELF.
CONGRATULATIONS, SIR.
WARNER BROTHERS IS NOW THE PROUD OWNER OF ATARI.

LIFE WAS GOOD.

SELLING ATARI FELT RIGHT. MOVING ON TO THE NEXT CHAPTER, THE NEXT FRONTIER!

PONG

THE GAME'S NOT OVER, NOLAN!

HUH? YOU STILL HERE?

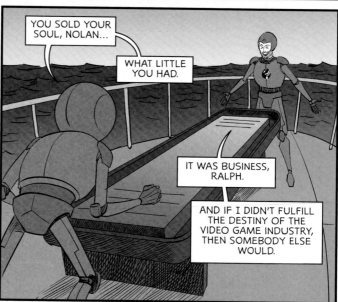

YOU SOLD YOUR SOUL, NOLAN...

WHAT LITTLE YOU HAD.

IT WAS BUSINESS, RALPH.

AND IF I DIDN'T FULFILL THE DESTINY OF THE VIDEO GAME INDUSTRY, THEN SOMEBODY ELSE WOULD.

HOW TRUE THAT IS, NOLAN.

HOW TRUE THAT IS.

TAK!

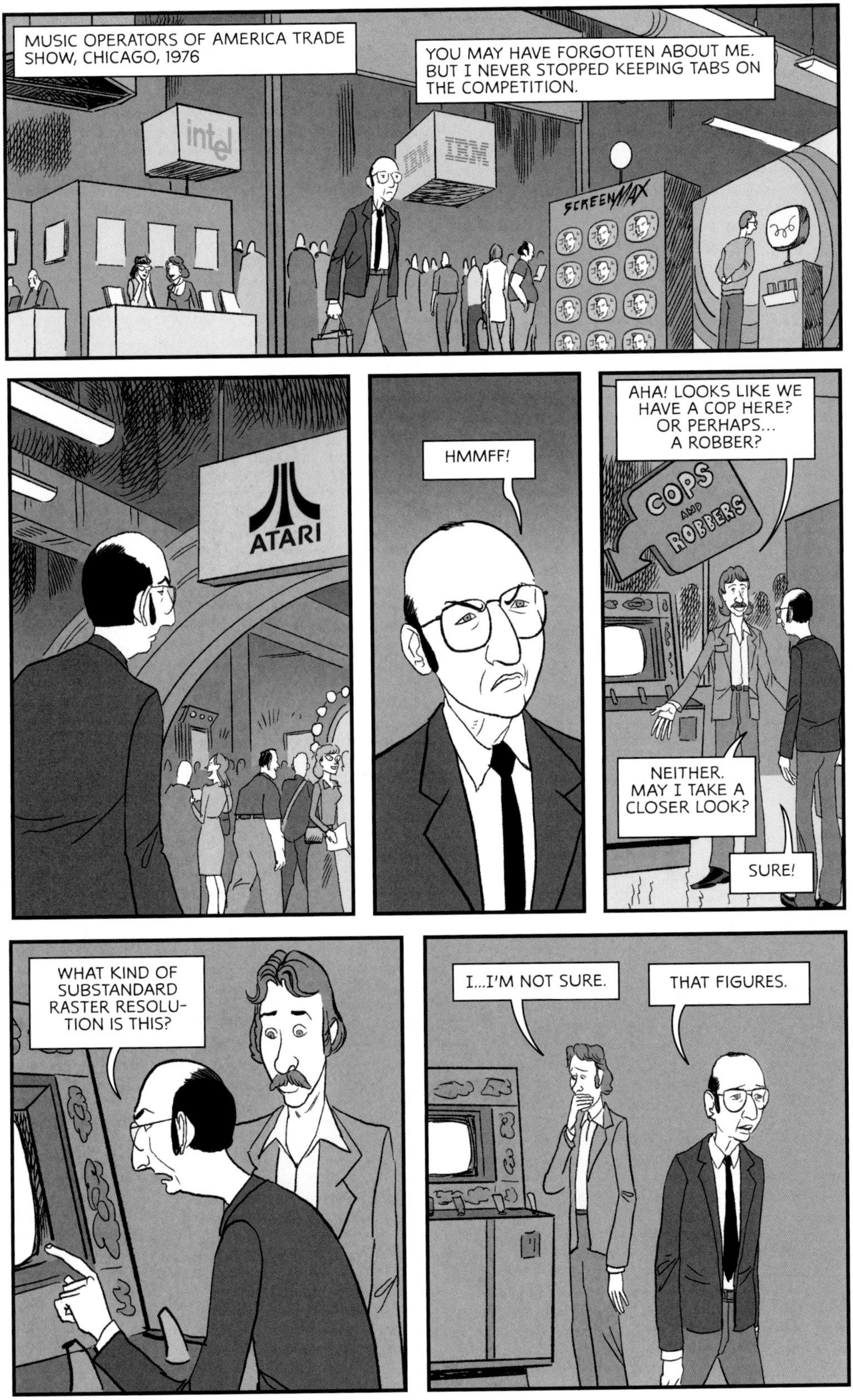
MUSIC OPERATORS OF AMERICA TRADE SHOW, CHICAGO, 1976
YOU MAY HAVE FORGOTTEN ABOUT ME. BUT I NEVER STOPPED KEEPING TABS ON THE COMPETITION.
intel
IBM
SCREENMAX
ATARI
HMMFF!
COPS AND ROBBERS
AHA! LOOKS LIKE WE HAVE A COP HERE? OR PERHAPS... A ROBBER?
NEITHER. MAY I TAKE A CLOSER LOOK?
SURE!
WHAT KIND OF SUBSTANDARD RASTER RESOLU-TION IS THIS?
I...I'M NOT SURE.
THAT FIGURES.

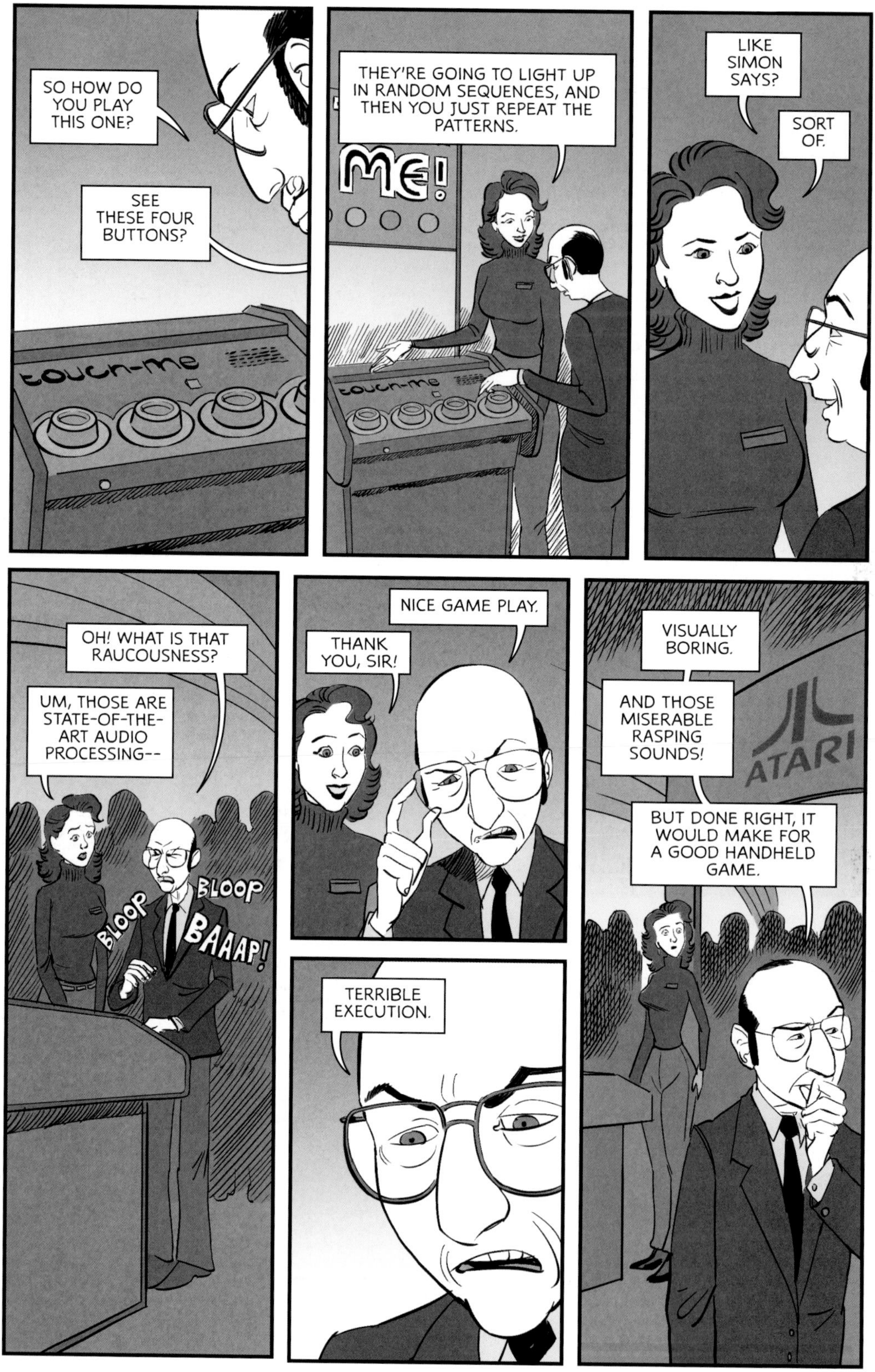
SO HOW DO YOU PLAY THIS ONE?
SEE THESE FOUR BUTTONS?
touch-me
THEY'RE GOING TO LIGHT UP IN RANDOM SEQUENCES, AND THEN YOU JUST REPEAT THE PATTERNS.
ME!
touch-me
LIKE SIMON SAYS?
SORT OF.
OH! WHAT IS THAT RAUCOUSNESS?
UM, THOSE ARE STATE-OF-THE-ART AUDIO PROCESSING--
BLOOP
BLOOP
BAAAP!
NICE GAME PLAY.
THANK YOU, SIR!
TERRIBLE EXECUTION.
VISUALLY BORING.
AND THOSE MISERABLE RASPING SOUNDS!
ATARI
BUT DONE RIGHT, IT WOULD MAKE FOR A GOOD HANDHELD GAME.

THE FOLLOWING WEEK

AS AN ENGINEER, I WAS ALWAYS LOOKING FOR NEW WAYS TO EXPLOIT THE LATEST TECHNOLOGIES.

WE CAN BUILD THE GAME AROUND THE TEXAS INSTRUMENTS TMS-1000 MICROPROCESSOR CHIP.

LIKE THE PRO-GRAMMABLE RECORD CHANGER I CODED?

PRECISELY.

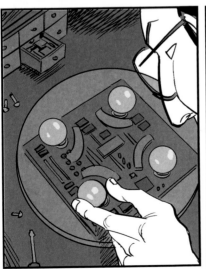

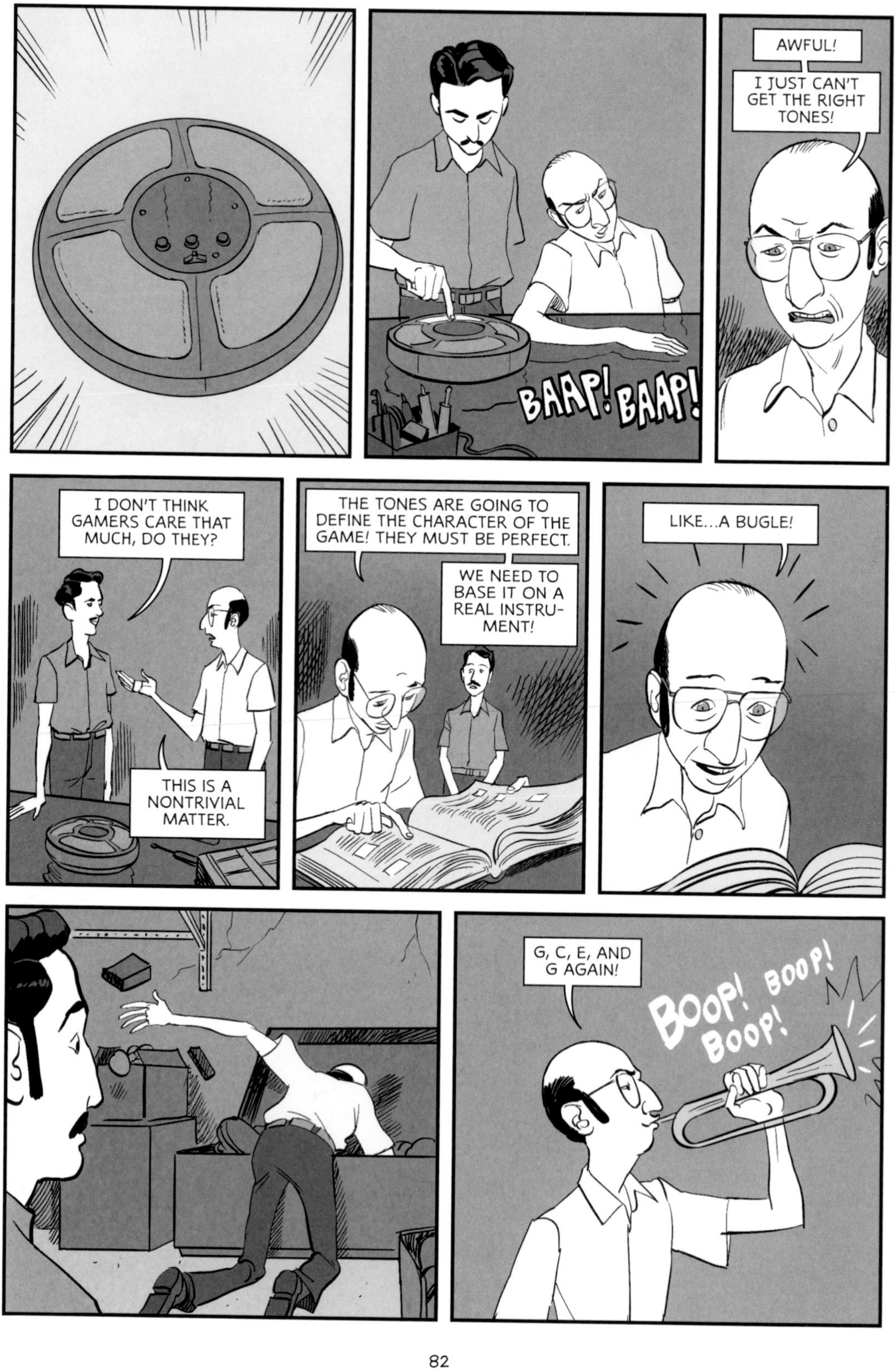
BAAP! BAAP!
AWFUL!
I JUST CAN'T GET THE RIGHT TONES!
I DON'T THINK GAMERS CARE THAT MUCH, DO THEY?
THIS IS A NONTRIVIAL MATTER.
THE TONES ARE GOING TO DEFINE THE CHARACTER OF THE GAME! THEY MUST BE PERFECT.
WE NEED TO BASE IT ON A REAL INSTRU-MENT!
LIKE...A BUGLE!
G, C, E, AND G AGAIN!
BOOP! BOOP! BOOP!

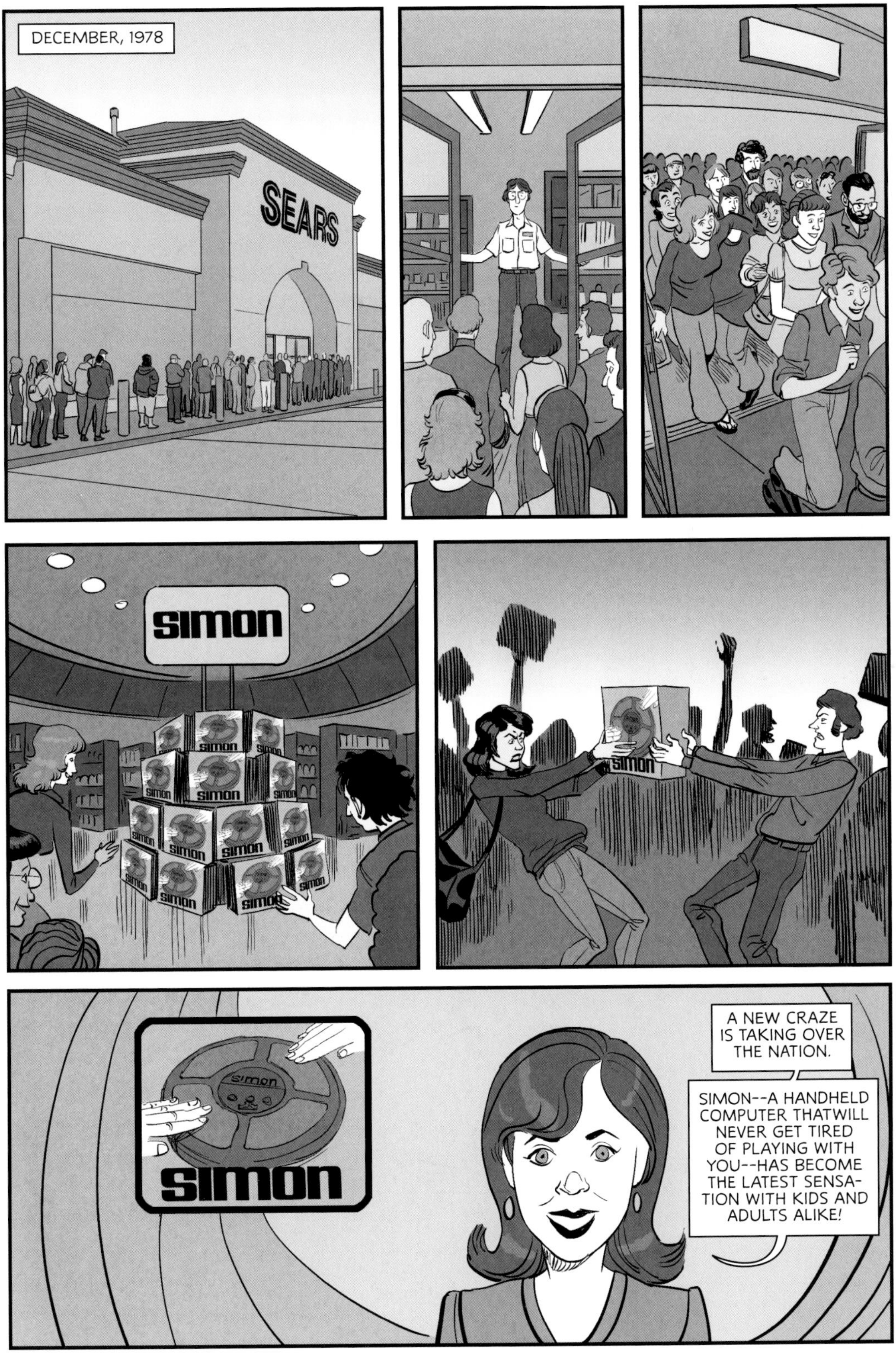
DECEMBER, 1978
SEARS
SIMON
SIMON
SIMON
SIMON
A NEW CRAZE IS TAKING OVER THE NATION.
SIMON--A HANDHELD COMPUTER THATWILL NEVER GET TIRED OF PLAYING WITH YOU--HAS BECOME THE LATEST SENSATION WITH KIDS AND ADULTS ALIKE!

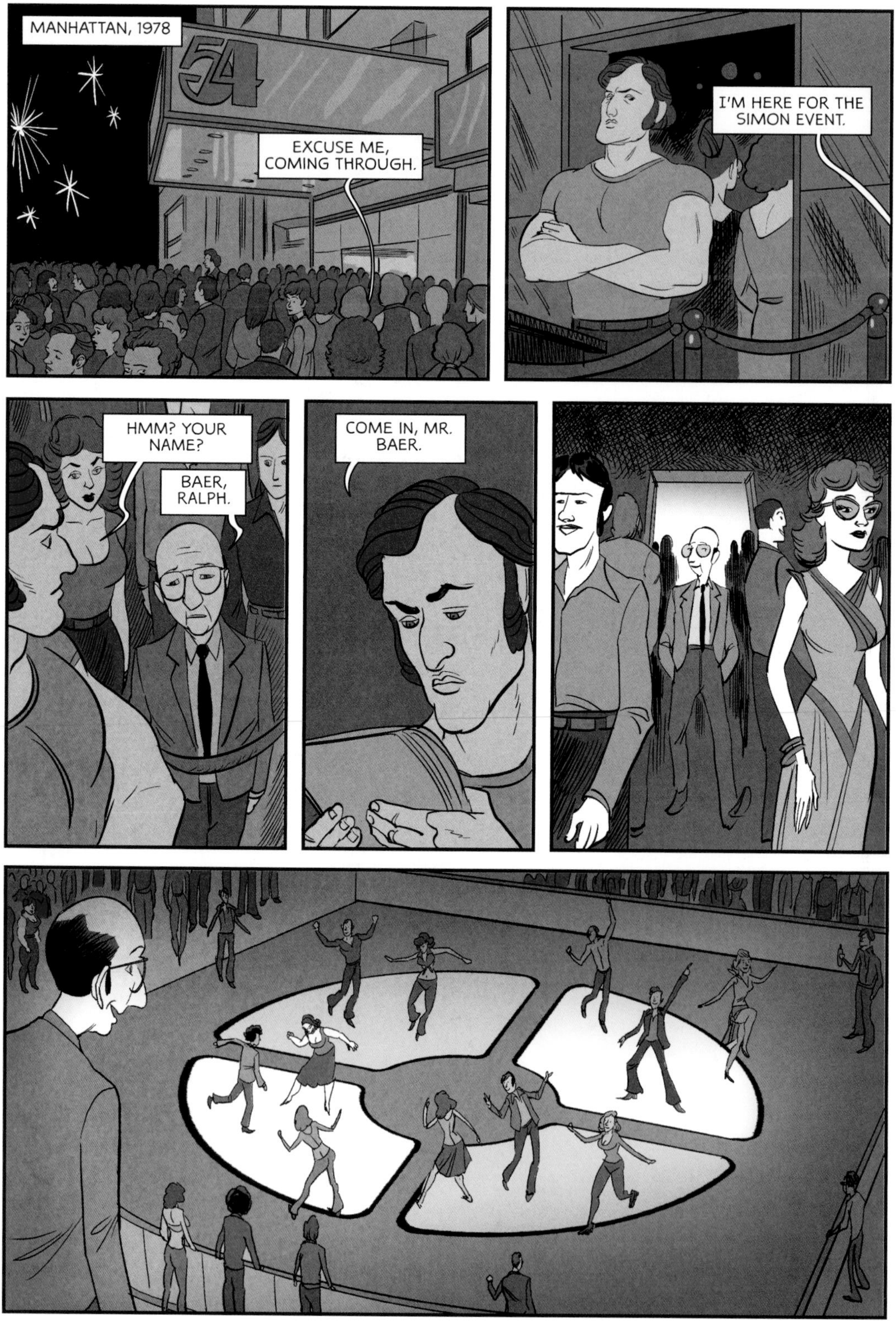
MANHATTAN, 1978
54
EXCUSE ME, COMING THROUGH.
I'M HERE FOR THE SIMON EVENT.
HMM? YOUR NAME?
BAER, RALPH.
COME IN, MR. BAER.

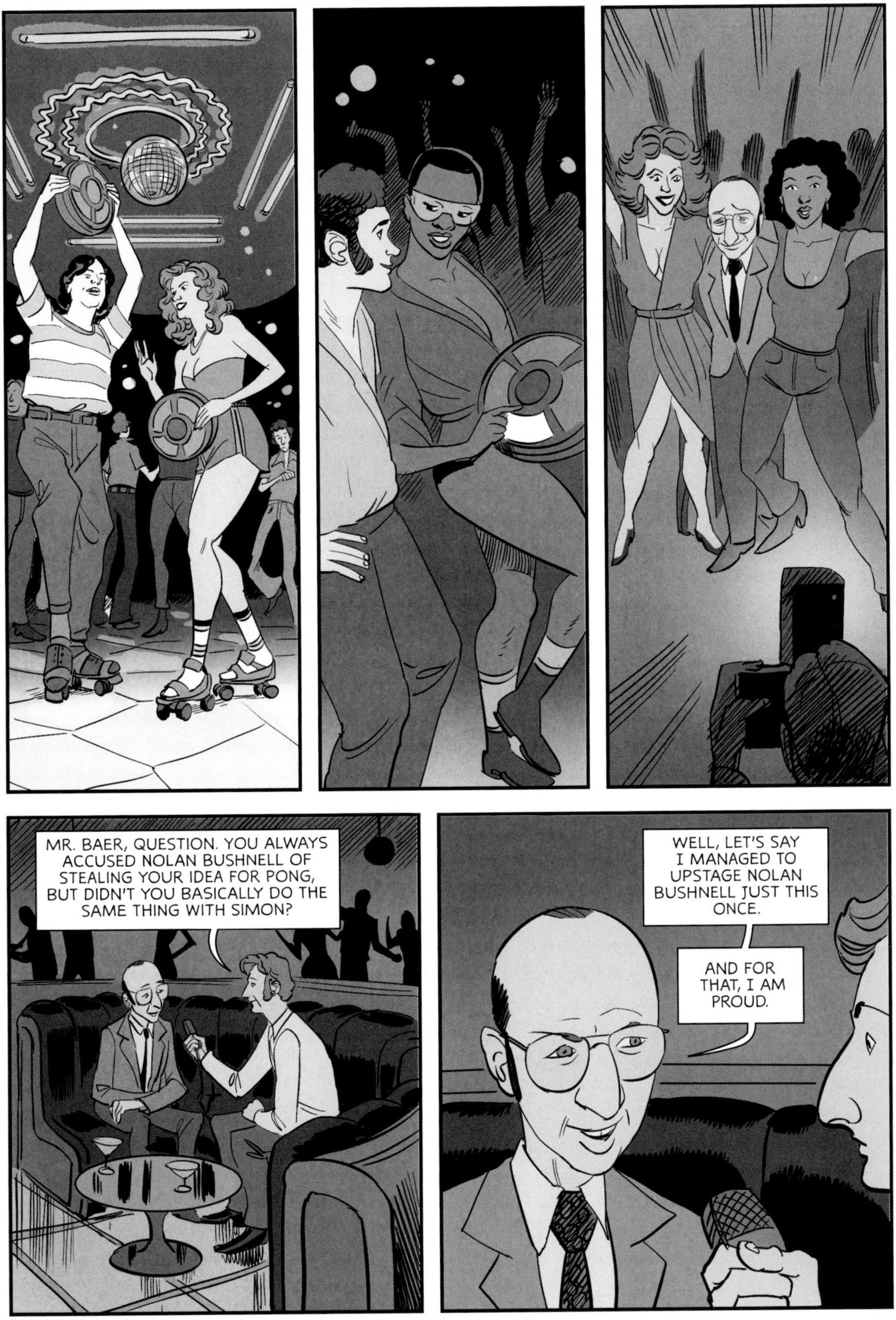
MR. BAER, QUESTION. YOU ALWAYS ACCUSED NOLAN BUSHNELL OF STEALING YOUR IDEA FOR PONG, BUT DIDN'T YOU BASICALLY DO THE SAME THING WITH SIMON?
WELL, LET'S SAY I MANAGED TO UPSTAGE NOLAN BUSHNELL JUST THIS ONCE.
AND FOR THAT, I AM PROUD.

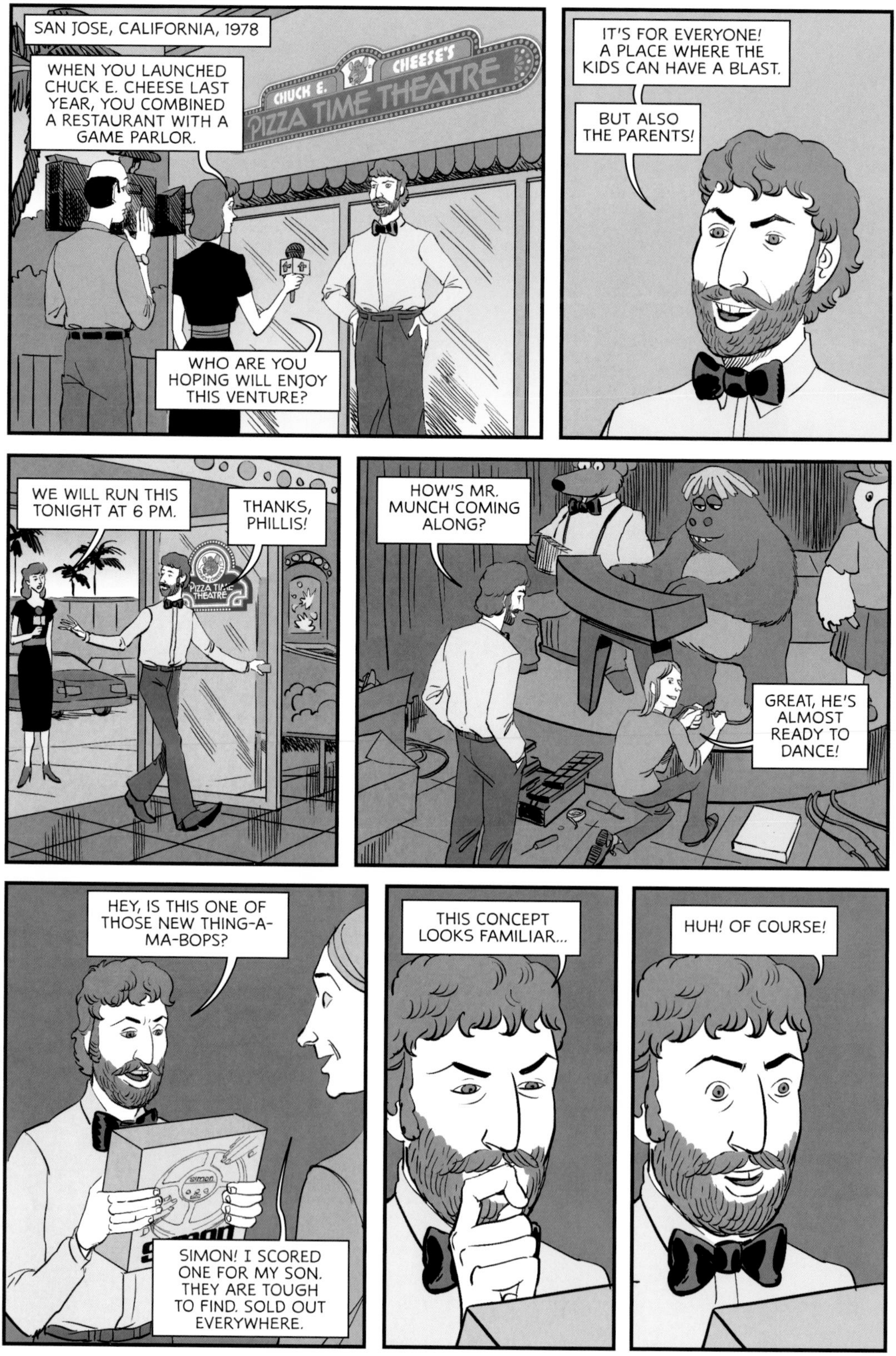
SAN JOSE, CALIFORNIA, 1978
WHEN YOU LAUNCHED CHUCK E. CHEESE LAST YEAR, YOU COMBINED A RESTAURANT WITH A GAME PARLOR.
CHUCK E. CHEESE'S PIZZA TIME THEATRE
WHO ARE YOU HOPING WILL ENJOY THIS VENTURE?
IT'S FOR EVERYONE! A PLACE WHERE THE KIDS CAN HAVE A BLAST.
BUT ALSO THE PARENTS!
WE WILL RUN THIS TONIGHT AT 6 PM.
THANKS, PHILLIS!
PIZZA TIME THEATRE
HOW'S MR. MUNCH COMING ALONG?
GREAT, HE'S ALMOST READY TO DANCE!
HEY, IS THIS ONE OF THOSE NEW THING-A-MA-BOPS?
SIMON! I SCORED ONE FOR MY SON. THEY ARE TOUGH TO FIND. SOLD OUT EVERYWHERE.
THIS CONCEPT LOOKS FAMILIAR...
HUH! OF COURSE!

40 YEARS LATER...

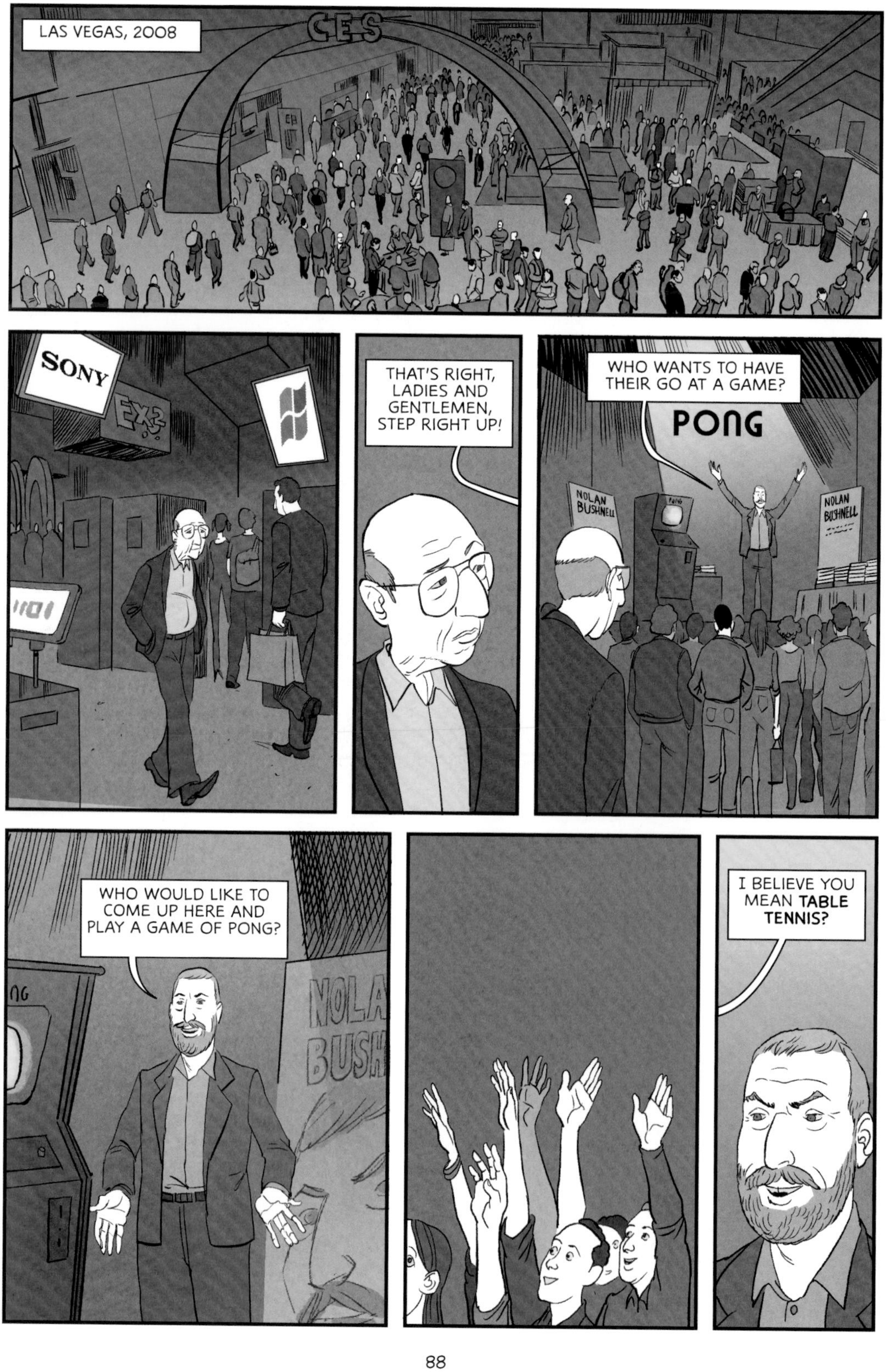
LAS VEGAS, 2008
CES
SONY
THAT'S RIGHT, LADIES AND GENTLEMEN, STEP RIGHT UP!
WHO WANTS TO HAVE THEIR GO AT A GAME?
PONG
NOLAN BUSHNELL
NOLAN BUSHNELL
WHO WOULD LIKE TO COME UP HERE AND PLAY A GAME OF PONG?
I BELIEVE YOU MEAN **TABLE TENNIS?**

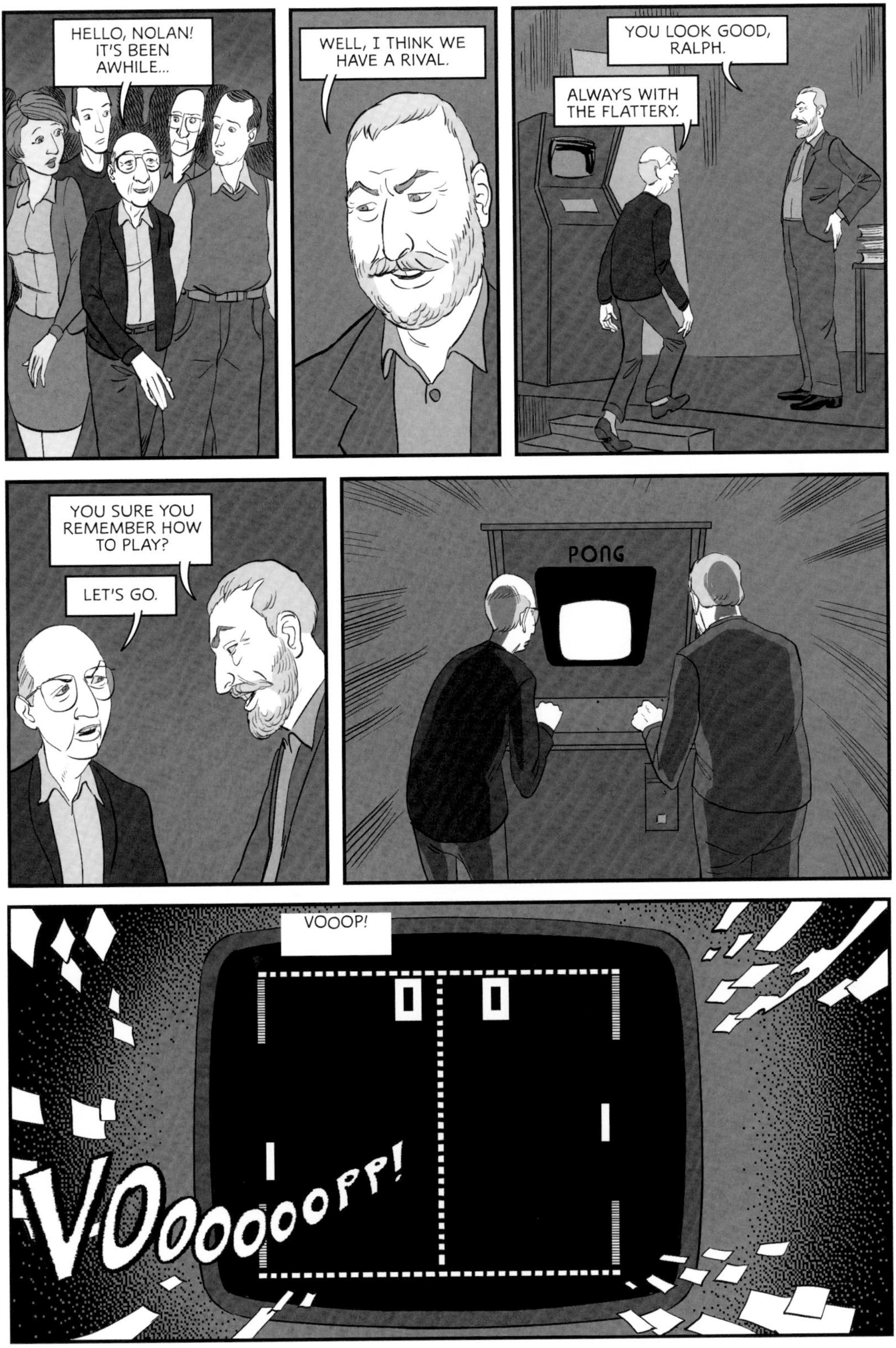
HELLO, NOLAN! IT'S BEEN AWHILE...
WELL, I THINK WE HAVE A RIVAL.
YOU LOOK GOOD, RALPH.
ALWAYS WITH THE FLATTERY.
YOU SURE YOU REMEMBER HOW TO PLAY?
LET'S GO.
PONG
VOOOP!
V-OOOOOOPP!

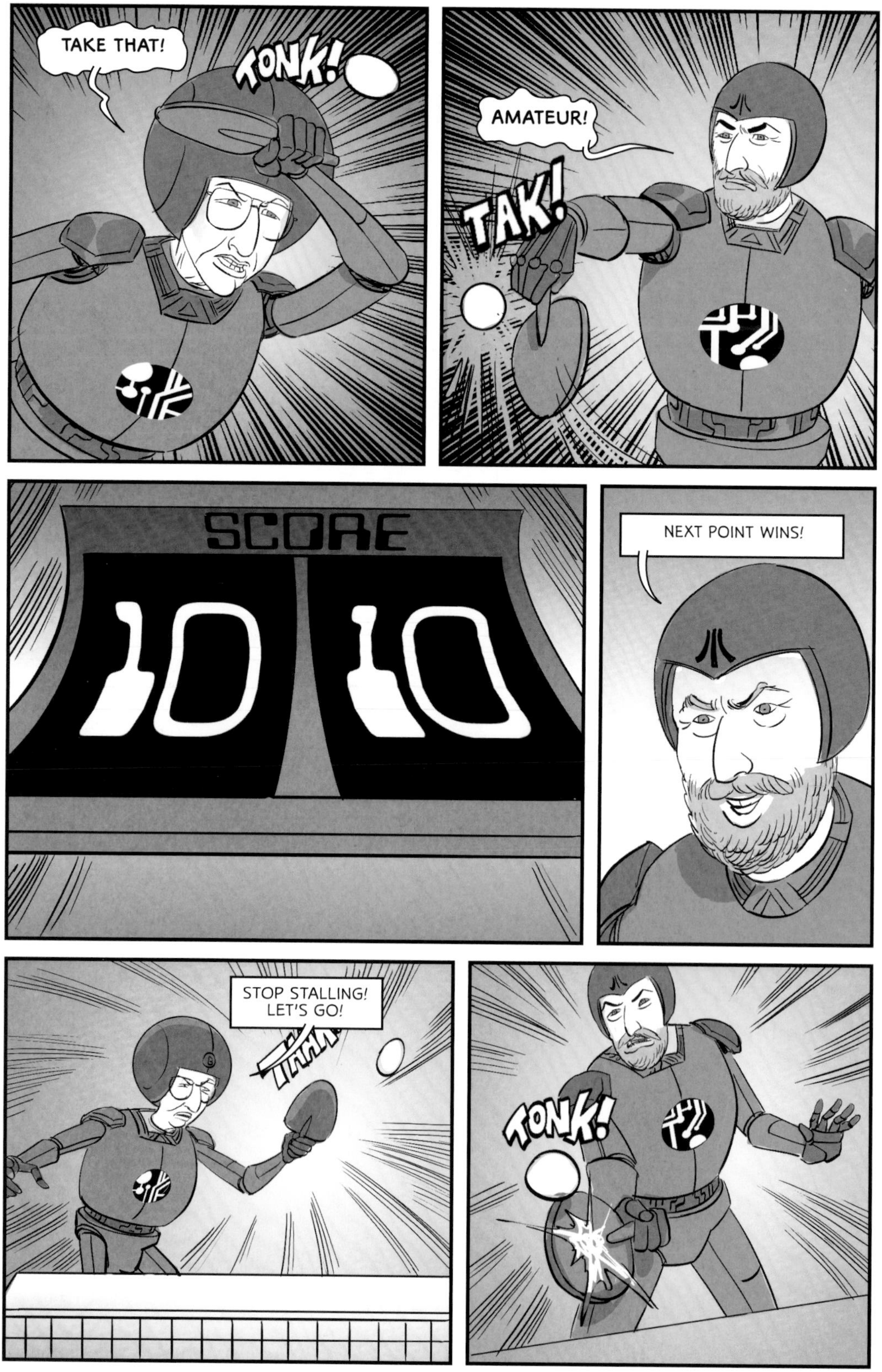

TAKE THAT!
TONK!
AMATEUR!
TAK!
SCORE
10
10
NEXT POINT WINS!
STOP STALLING! LET'S GO!
TONK!

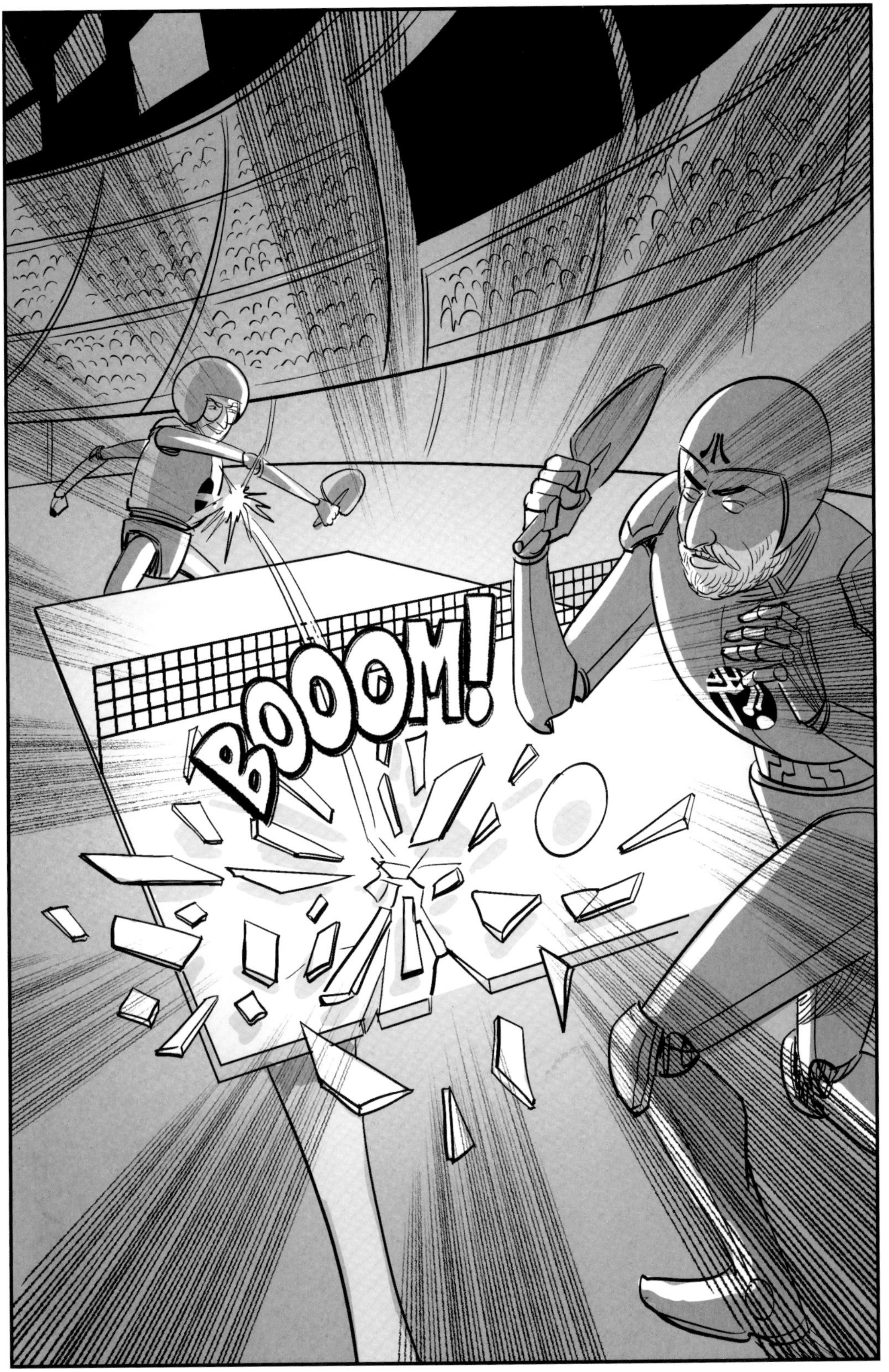
BOOOM!

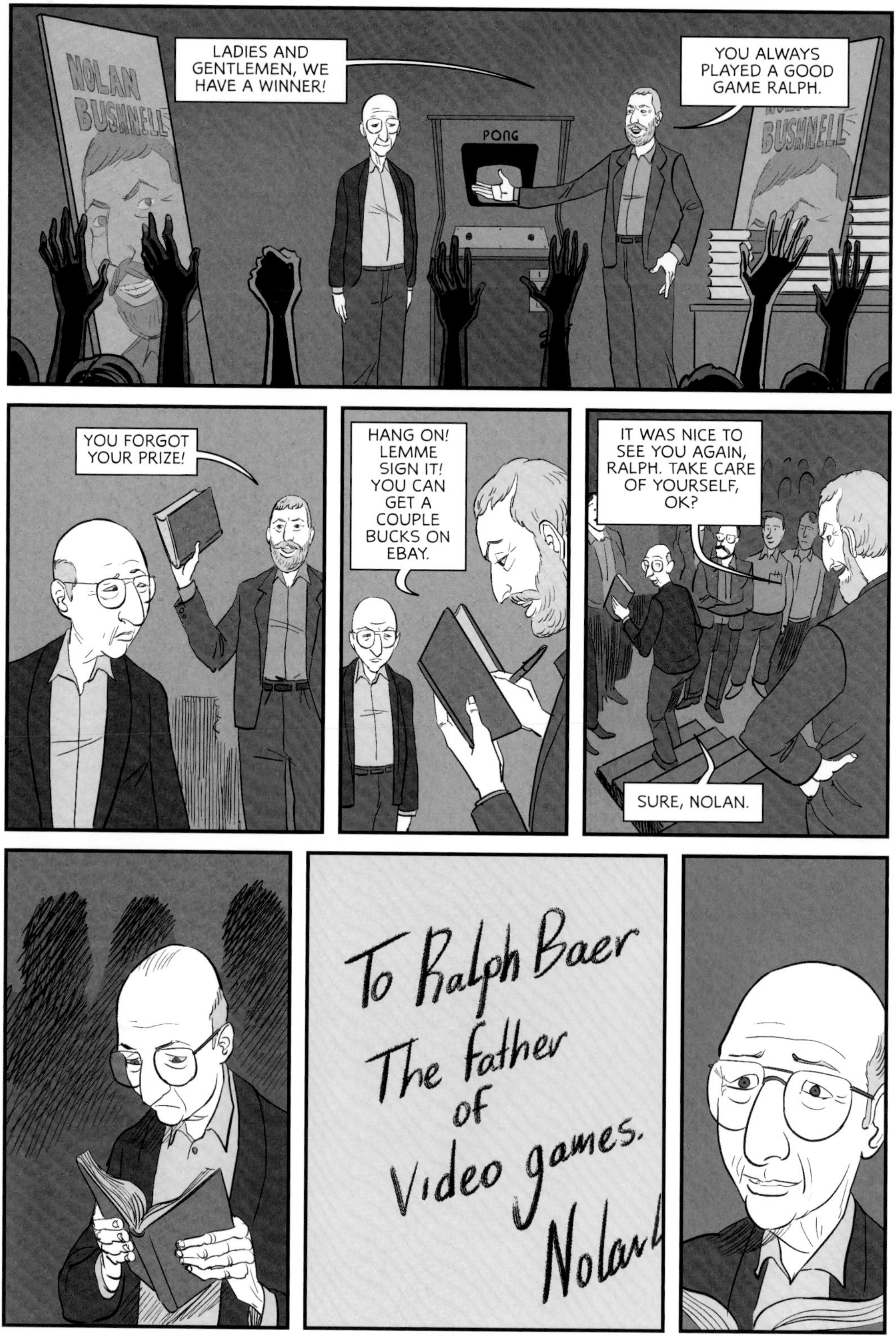
NOLAN BUSHNELL
LADIES AND GENTLEMEN, WE HAVE A WINNER!
PONG
YOU ALWAYS PLAYED A GOOD GAME RALPH.
BUSHNELL
YOU FORGOT YOUR PRIZE!
HANG ON! LEMME SIGN IT! YOU CAN GET A COUPLE BUCKS ON EBAY.
IT WAS NICE TO SEE YOU AGAIN, RALPH. TAKE CARE OF YOURSELF, OK?
SURE, NOLAN.
To Ralph Baer
The father
of
Video games.
Nolan

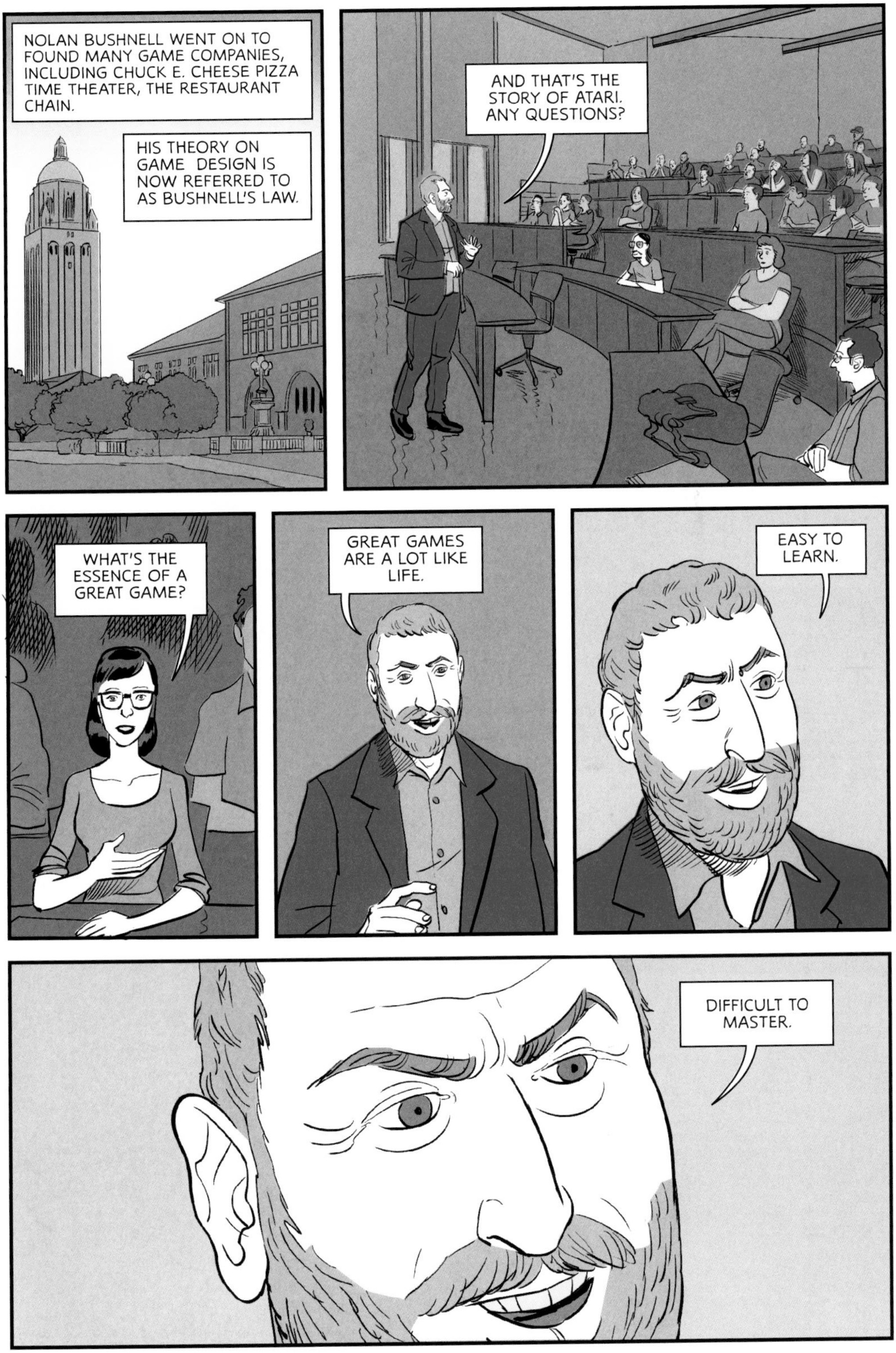
NOLAN BUSHNELL WENT ON TO FOUND MANY GAME COMPANIES, INCLUDING CHUCK E. CHEESE PIZZA TIME THEATER, THE RESTAURANT CHAIN.
HIS THEORY ON GAME DESIGN IS NOW REFERRED TO AS BUSHNELL'S LAW.
AND THAT'S THE STORY OF ATARI. ANY QUESTIONS?
WHAT'S THE ESSENCE OF A GREAT GAME?
GREAT GAMES ARE A LOT LIKE LIFE.
EASY TO LEARN.
DIFFICULT TO MASTER.

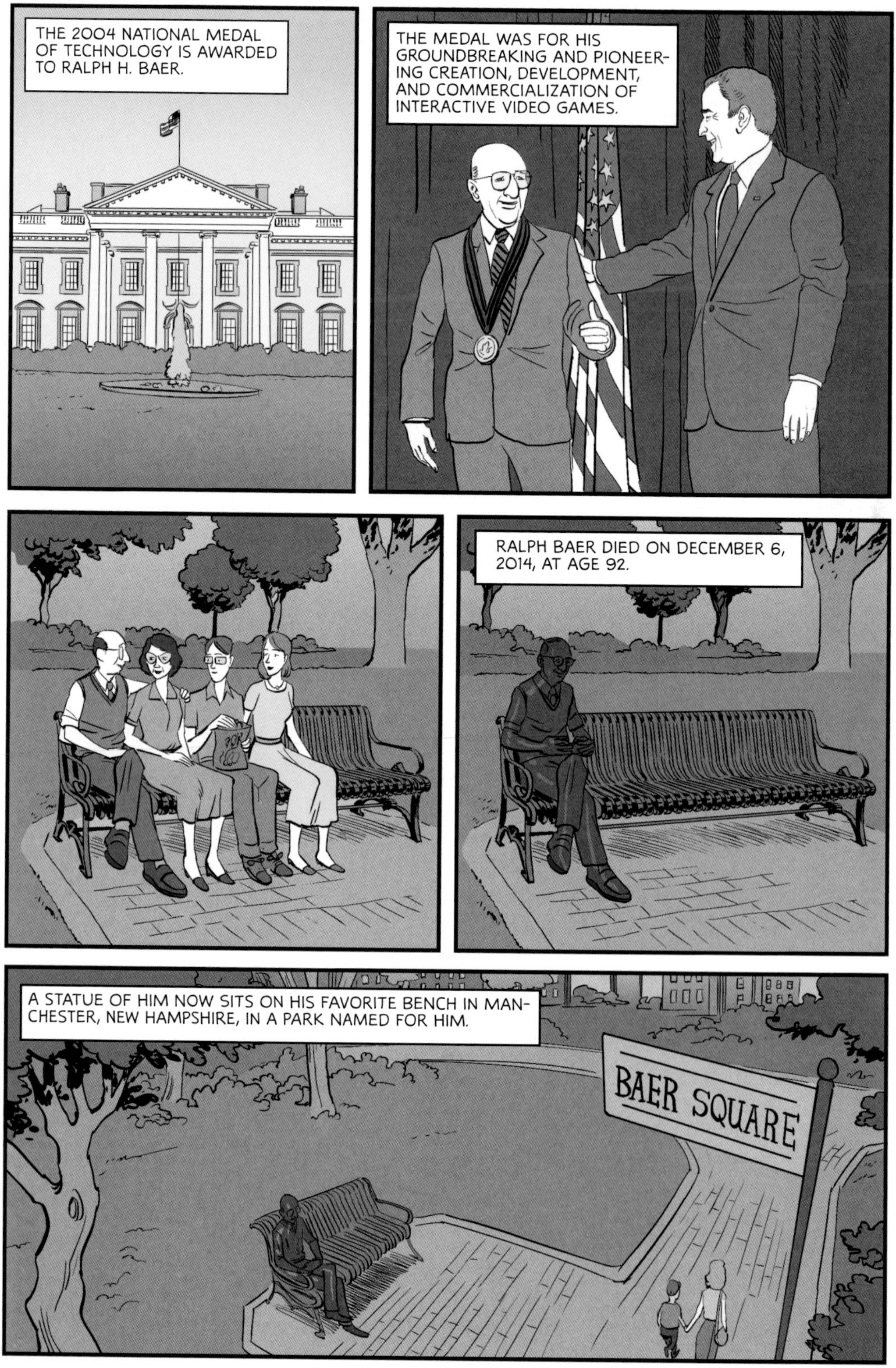
THE 2004 NATIONAL MEDAL OF TECHNOLOGY IS AWARDED TO RALPH H. BAER.
THE MEDAL WAS FOR HIS GROUNDBREAKING AND PIONEERING CREATION, DEVELOPMENT, AND COMMERCIALIZATION OF INTERACTIVE VIDEO GAMES.
RALPH BAER DIED ON DECEMBER 6, 2014, AT AGE 92.
A STATUE OF HIM NOW SITS ON HIS FAVORITE BENCH IN MANCHESTER, NEW HAMPSHIRE, IN A PARK NAMED FOR HIM.
BAER SQUARE

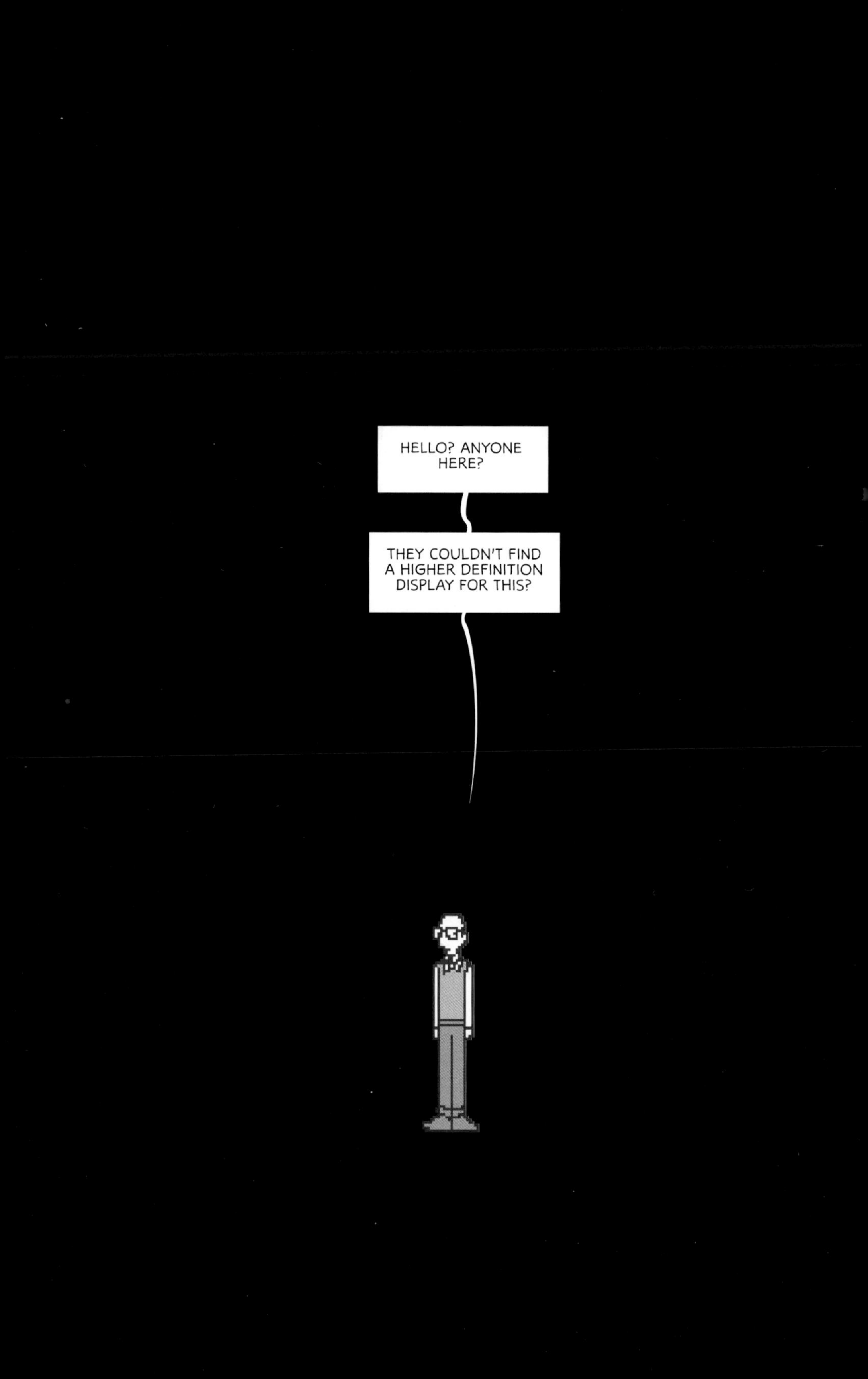
HELLO? ANYONE HERE?
THEY COULDN'T FIND A HIGHER DEFINITION DISPLAY FOR THIS?

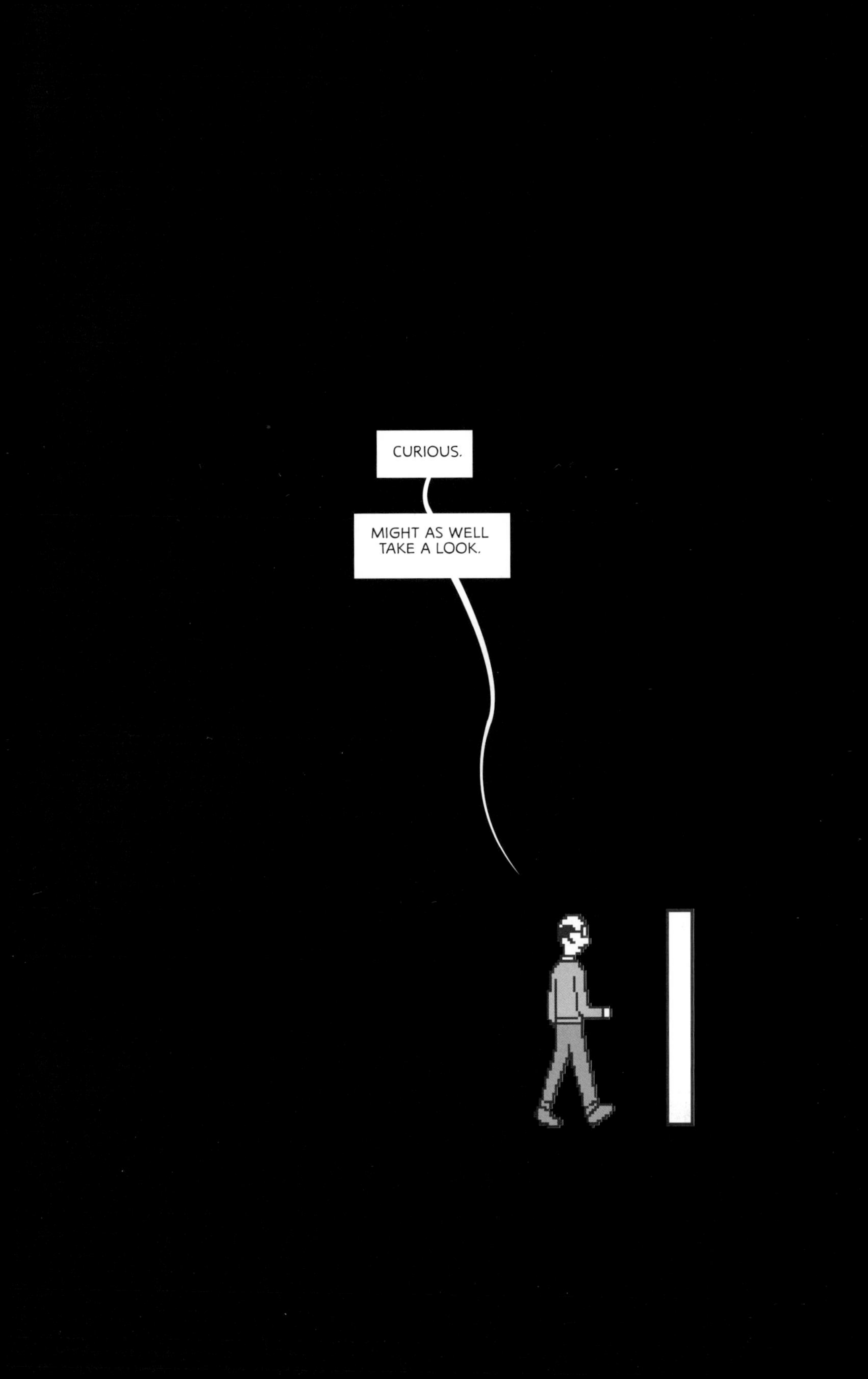
CURIOUS.
MIGHT AS WELL TAKE A LOOK.

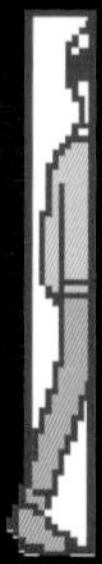

ABOUT THE AUTHORS

© Gasper Tringale

© Mary Abramson

DAVID KUSHNER, AN AWARD-WINNING AUTHOR AND JOURNALIST, AND **KOREN SHADMI**, AN ILLUSTRATOR AND CARTOONIST, ARE COAUTHORS OF *RISE OF THE DUNGEON MASTER* AND *A FOR ANONYMOUS.*